Old Testament Stories

What Do They Say Today?

Joe E. Morris, Ph.D. &
Roy H. Ryan, D.Min.

CROSSLINK
PUBLISHING

Old Testament Stories: What Do They Say Today?

꠿ CrossLink Publishing
꠿ www.crosslink.org

ISBN 978-1-936746-22-4

Table of Contents

Preface

When our youngest son had seen Star Wars for the twelfth or thirteenth time, I said, "Why do you go so often?" He said, "For the same reason you have been reading the Old Testament all of your life."

The stories of the Old Testament always draw our attention. A mysterious spirit broods over dark waters and the earth rises majestically from foaming, misty waters; heaven lowers like a large crystal dome and sun, moon and stars appear as if evoked by an artist's deft touch. A human is formed from the dust of the earth and his mate fashioned miraculously from one of his ribs. A mighty flood covers the earth and a man with a gigantic boat saves humankind and all living creatures big and small. A skyscraper reaching to the heavens separates people and causes them to speak different languages. A shepherd boy kills a giant with a sling shot and becomes king. A huge fish swallows a man and in three days coughs him up. We could go on and on.

These biblical stories are the stories we heard as children. They grabbed our attention in our first Sunday school classes. Their pictures were our first images of faith. In those years of innocence these stories gave us hope and courage. They nurtured our fledging beliefs. We passed them along to our children with the hope they will pass them to their children and continue passing them, generation upon generation until the end of time.

Millennia ago, before they were written for the world to read, these great stories first appeared orally as songs and poems. They were sung and spoken around oasis campfires, in desert tents, in small villages beneath sycamore and oak trees. They were filled with wisdom, hope, encouragement, and guidance for a nomadic people. These wanderers began to cluster into small villages that eventually grew into towns and cities. Generation to generation, the stories grew with the people and the messages became part of their faith tradition. In those days, the stories were vibrant and alive. They *were* the Word of the Lord.

Today, four millennia later, the stories are still read and revered by people of faith. They stir our imaginations. The magnetism that draws Bill Moyer's son to *Star Wars* over and over is one reason we continue to read the ancient stories of the Bible. But are they the vibrant Word of God they were long ago? Do they still speak today? If so, what do they say? The story-lines are active but do the messages of God's word still resonate? Are they merely a collection of old stories about God's mighty acts that no longer relate to the twenty-first century? Will they continue to be passed from generation to generation until the end of time or will they eventually die the slow death of a malnourished, anemic traditionalism? Will they continue to be easy bedtime reads for youngsters who will later grapple with the contradictions and inconsistencies and decide to trash them? Will future generations decide these stories belong to a pre-scientific age and have no relevance for their lives? Is writer and scholar Joseph Campbell correct when he says, "The old time religion belongs to another age, another people, another set of human values, another universe."

Based upon modern trends these stories continue to be read, but the average reader may be missing the power of their spiritual truths. The end result is a lack of interest in the theology of the stories. For this reason, some branches of modern Christianity give little attention to the Old Testament. How did this lack of interest in the Old Testament stories occur and what can we do to revitalize interest?

One reason these Old Testament stories are an endangered species relates to how they have been presented and interpreted over time. They have been portrayed as historical fact which most are not. Historical truth surfaces in some of them but the stories have little to do with history. They were intended to be vehicles of faith, testaments of belief. *The Old Testament* is not entitled *A History of the Israelites. The New Testament* is not entitled *A History of the Early Christian Church.* Because they are witnesses of faith, they are appropriately, and accurately, called *testaments.* These narrative accounts were never intended to be understood as fact, but as vehicles of spiritual truth, as testaments of faith by their respective "clouds of witnesses."

When presented as fact, these stories create unrealistic expectations. Young believers grow up and eventually face a choice. They can debunk and dump the stories as falsehoods, an unfortunate contemporary misunderstanding of myth, or they can adopt a literalistic position and incorporate the stories into their belief system as hard fact. The latter choice is intellectually dishonest and often leads to disillusion.

We believe these old stories are as relevant and meaningful now as they were millennia ago. We believe the messages are still there, as vibrant and poignant as they were when first sung, spoken, or written. To maintain their effectiveness, these stories must continually be interpreted for each generation.

The stories have been selected according to their popularity across time and the messages we considered most relevant for our age. Except for the story of Daniel, which follows Jonah, they are presented in the order they appear in the Old Testament. Linkage, a key word, is evidenced in that order. Common themes pervade these stories and continue into the New Testament, the reason Daniel is placed last. One objective of this book is to demonstrate how the truths of the stories of old found new life in the New Testament and can continue to be revitalized in the 21st century. Another is to bring the Old Testament back into the mainstream of Christian discussion, education and preaching. Targeted audiences include pastors and lay persons within the structure of the local church. Field-tested with several groups of different makeup, the book has already demonstrated an appeal to those with religious conservative backgrounds as well as those who have rejected the old interpretations and are looking for something fresh. Anyone who is searching for a deeper meaning and greater spiritual growth and development will find enriching insights and revelations.

This book can be read for personal knowledge and meditation or used as a teaching tool with small groups. The structure of each chapter is straightforward and simple: The Text, The Context, The Message, and Further Questions for Reflection and Discussion. With some stories, such as Ruth, Esther, and Jonah, a thematic format works best. The division subtitle "The Text" is the scripture. In some cases, due to the length of some scriptures, "The Text" will consist of key passages within the larger scripture. "The Context" discusses the history and background of the story, its placement within a larger text and relationship to other parts of the Old Testament. Context is also to how passages interweave into one body and interrelate. "The Message" flows from "The Context. "Questions for Reflection and Discussion" are provided at the end of each chapter for personal meditation /or group study.

Because most of us are creatures of habit, another issue that generates some concern among Christians is the shift in dividing time from B. C. and A. D. to B. C. E. (Before the Common Era) and C. E. (Common Era). We Christians must realize, and rally understanding, that for those of other faiths—Jews, Muslims, Buddhists, etc.—Jesus is not Lord and the abbreviations which work well for us, lack meaning and relevance for them. For this reason, most scholars have begun using the more inclusive abbreviations. Therefore "Common Era" means common to all people of all faiths who use the calendar of Western civilization and "B.C.E." means "Before the Common Era." The newer trend will be followed in this book.

For purposes of consistency and continuity, we have chosen the *New International Version* (NIV) of the Old Testament. However, we encourage our readers to read the same scripture from *The King James Version* (KJV), the *Revised Standard Version* (REV), *New English Bible* (NEB) and or the version of their choice. Translations can represent particular viewpoints.

Chapter One

The First Creation Story: Heavens and Earth

Genesis 1-2:4a

THE TEXT

> In the beginning God created the heavens and the earth.
> Now the earth was formless and empty, darkness was
> over the surface of the deep and the Spirit of God was
> hovering over the waters. And God said, "Let there be
> light," and there was light. God saw that the light was
> good, and he separated the light from the darkness. God
> called the light "day," and the darkness he called "night."
> And there was evening and there was morning—the first day.
>
> —Genesis 1: 1-5

THE CONTEXT

The scripture cited above is from the *New International Version.*
The version most of us remember is from the *King James Bible*. The
story appears at the very beginning of the Bible and is the one we
heard first and know by heart. It is possibly the only creation story in
our biblical memory. On the second day, God created the waters and
the sky, and on the third day he created vegetation, plants, and trees of
every kind. The sun, moon, and stars were created on the fourth day
and living creatures on the fifth. Man was created on the sixth day.
Then scripture states, **Thus the heavens and the earth were
completed in all their vast array**, (2:1) and God rested.

In this first story of creation, there is no primordial struggle or combat. From the beginning, God is in control. He is working from a determined plan. He is sovereign master of the universe, giving direction by verbal commands: **God said, 'Let there be light,' and there was light.** (Genesis 1:3) He is finished in six days and rests on the seventh.

From the second verse on, God's spiritual presence is dominant: **The Spirit of God was hovering over the waters.** The primary cause of the creation is God's spiritual presence, not his voice. His voice is but an extension of His Spirit. This symbolic image of a spirit-filled God breathing his creating spirit into us as he hovers above persists throughout the Old and into the New Testament, throughout the life of the early church and into our present day.

THE MESSAGE

What does a biblical story in which God creates the earth in six days and rests have to say to the 21st century? More than any story in the Bible, this creation story collides with modern science and contemporary thought. After reading Genesis 1-5, many conclude this part of the Bible has nothing to say today. The story is millennia removed from our world of outer space, cyber space, and MySpace. However, when we examine these stories within context and in light of other biblical references, significant truths emerge.

In the beginning God...

Whether in the centuries B.C.E. or in the 21st century C.E., all Judeo-Christian beliefs rest upon this one premise. **In the beginning God** is the beginning of theology as well as of philosophy. Ancient and modern philosophers ask the ultimate question of being: Why is there something rather than nothing? The authors of the creation story answer: **In the beginning God.** This is fundamental. There is either some viable, creative force behind this grand scheme or there is not. All faith begins with this core belief or it is empty and meaningless. Without an ultimate creator God, Lord of the Universe, there would have been no rainbow after the Flood, no faith of Abraham, no Promised Land, no Exodus, no deliverance from bondage, no burning bush, no Israel, Davidic dynasty, or messianic vision…no Christ…no resurrection. Without **In the beginning God,** the entire structures of creed and dogma, ritual and liturgy would collapse.

The times in which we live are as precarious and shaky as those of old. The universe hangs by a thread. A wandering comet, aberrant meteoroid, or wayward meteorite could come crashing into our lives and end our revels, leave our world…

> …melted into air, into thin air;
>
> And like the baseless fabric of this vision,
>
> The cloud-capp'd towers, the gorgeous palaces,
>
> The solemn temples, the great globe itself,
>
> Yea, all which it inherit, shall dissolve
>
> And like this insubstantial pageant faded,
>
> Leave not a rack behind.[1]

When we affirm, "We believe in God the Father…" we declare our belief in a Supreme Being and Creator. Through our creed, based upon Genesis 1:1, we affirm God's existence. There was never a time God did not exist. Though we are born into existence, God was never born. He was always *there*. God could never "not exist." Beyond the deep chaotic abyss an eternal God has always existed. God's love has always been the heart of the universe.

In the beginning God…The writer John surely thought of this when composing the Prologue to his Gospel: "In the beginning was the Word." (1:1) He knew that without this Ultimate, creative and sustaining Force, he could not finish his Gospel. The papyrus leaves would be blank; the ink would dry up. There would be no Christ to write about if it were not for **In the beginning God.** There would be no Trinity or Triune God.

The writers of Old Testament Wisdom literature knew this. The Creation held a central position. It was an absolute basis for faith. The history of Israel is a saving history and it begins with a "saving"

3

creation. The theme resonates in the prologue of the Gospel of John and throughout the New Testament.

The belief in one God, Monotheism, was the guiding force in the faith development of the People of God, later known as "The People of Israel." The creation story affirmed that One God, known as YHWH (the Hebrew language left out vowels), which has come to be known as Yahweh, was the life force for all of the created order, including humankind. The story helped the Hebrews believe in this One and only, powerful God, with whom they were bound by a Covenant Relationship.

In the beginning God created...and God saw that it was good. (1:1, 10b)

Often what is not said in scripture looms more important than what is said. God is not depicted saying "it was the best" or "it was perfect." He did not sit back with a satisfied sultanic clap and say, "It is finished." Whether one believes the earth was created in six literal days or in six days symbolic of a much lengthier time frame, God took his time. An intrinsic value of goodness exists in all of creation. But it was not perfected. St. Paul spoke of "the whole creation as groaning," just as we ourselves groan inwardly for redemption. (Romans 8:22). Creation is good but it can be better. God has given to us a wondrous and ample creation for all of our physical needs, but His "good" creation was not an end product. It was the beginning of one which would continue. Creation is on-going and humans are involved with God in the process. The writer of the first Genesis creation story makes this clear as he quickly moves to the theme of stewardship: **...let them rule...over all the earth and over all the creatures...(1:26).**

God has appointed us stewards of His creation. As people in covenant with the Creator God, we are called to care for the earth and all of creation. The Old Testament story of creation, what does it say today? It speaks volumes, relevant and timely volumes. No Old Testament theme could be more relevant to today's world.

A critical part of that stewardship is stated in Genesis 1:26, **And God said 'Let us make humankind in our own image, according to our likeness and let them have dominion over the fish of the sea and the birds of the air...over all the earth.** We are enough like God

4

that we can think, we can plan, we can analyze, etc. Therefore, we have the capacity to take care of the creation that God has given to us. Being made in God's image means we must assume God-like responsibilities. That is the challenge implied. Granted, it was His world, but we are made in His image and granted the responsibility of being His stewards.

Whether one believes in creationism or evolution, **In the beginning was God...and God saw that it was good.** God was the divine creating, driving force. Regardless of one's religious orientation, there is a growing concern among people of faith to support global conservation. Jews and Christians, Fundamentalists and Liberals, all join in supporting policies and practices of conservation, globally and locally. In our local community, recycling has become a part of daily routine. As we take our recyclable items to the street on "recycling day" we feel we are fulfilling a challenge inscribed millennia ago in the first verses of the Bible. When one of our councilwomen suggested recycling was our "Christian duty," she was blasted by others on the newspaper's editorial page. Some saw no connection with Christ or with the Christ of the Trinity, co-creator with "God the Father, maker of heaven and earth." They had probably never heard of the first heresy of the church which denied responsibility for anything material. They had never heard of Gnostics. But their reactions mirror the first heresy the early church faced.

The question is as valid now as ever: What is God's will for creation today? If we are to believe the first verses of the Bible, we can rest assured God wills for the creation to serve the highest purposes of humankind and for humankind to reciprocate. If we are to believe the first verses of the Bible, we can rest assured God does not *will* waste and destruction. The contemporary concern for "Global warming" is certainly one way of understanding what our wastefulness is doing to the planet.

How can we work with God to bring about a better quality of stewardship to avoid endangering creation? A slogan recently made the rounds among environmentalists and those tuned to environmental issues: "Live simply that others may simply live." This phrase becomes more and more meaningful as we consider famine around the world Darfur, Somalia, Bangladesh—where people cannot grow their own food. What should people of faith do? There is the ever-present growing energy crisis. Should we use corn, needed by starving millions, to make ethanol to help reduce our dependency on foreign crude oil? What should people of faith do? Should we make sacrifices, drive slower, drive less, car pool, use mass transit, etc., etc.? What is God's will for creation? Should people of faith make personal sacrifices so starving children thousands of miles away can live, live more simply that they might simply live?

We have been wasteful. Our actions are slowly destroying the fragile biosphere, "the heavens," that protects us, that God said was "good." We are using our natural resources as if they are limitless. Americans are conspicuous consumers. When will we learn? When will we take global warming seriously as a nation and become better stewards of God's "good" creation? When will we listen to ancient Bible verses that still speak today?

The Sabbath

By the seventh day God had finished the work he had been doing, so on the seventh day he rested from all his work. (2:2)

God rested. The most compelling aspect of this passage is God's humanness, a foreshadowing of Jesus when he grew weary and had to rest. (John 4:6) God was the first person to practice stress management. He maintained balance in his energy. This harmony is underscored in the following verse: **And God blessed the seventh day and made it holy.** But that is not the end of the thought. **God blessed the seventh day and made it holy *because* on it he rested from all his work of creating that he had done.** (2:3—italics added) Rest and holy are inextricably bound together. They are inseparably intertwined in the ongoing creative process. One cannot exist without the other. Work and rest are a rhythm in the created order of things. The concept is so important it is included in the Ten Commandments. Humans must honor this God-created, God-endowed rhythm. It is one as sensitive to disruption as the God-created, God-endowed ecosystem.

The word holy, as the great Scottish preacher James S. Stewart reminds us, may have lost its meaning. In his book *The Gates of New*

Life, Stewart credits the famous Baptist preacher Harry Emerson Fosdick for reminding us of the original meaning of the word.

> Wholesome, healthy. Holiness means inward health.
>
> It means healthy instincts, healthy emotions, every
>
> part of life in a disciplined, balanced, wholesome
>
> condition. It means, in short, to put it psychologically,
>
> an integrated personality.[2]

Holiness in individuals is achieved when they maintain a healthy integrated personality rather than striving to be pious, righteous, and set apart. One reaches a sense of balance in life which includes rest. The words of an old hymn call our attention to the importance of spending quiet time with God: "Take Time To Be Holy." If the omnipotent Creator in whose image we are made rested, should not we? Some faith groups observe other days for rest. According to the words of Jesus: "The Sabbath was made for man, not man for the Sabbath." (Mark 2:27) and "Therefore, it is lawful to do good on the Sabbath" (Matthew 12:12b; Mark 3:4; Luke 6: 9).

Holistic health is a concept that has come of age. Books on the subject are best-sellers and fill the Spiritual and Health sections at bookstores. People want to feel good and stay healthy. All of us need to be reminded that this is not only new news, it is old news, and it is good news.

QUESTIONS FOR FURTHER STUDY AND DISCUSSION

1. How did the Hebrew people arrive at a faith in One God? Why are the creation stories important to our understanding of God?
2. If all that God created "is good", does that mean creation is perfect? Do you believe that God created all of life and then left us to our devices? Or, is God still involved with us in His creative process?
3. How can we fulfill our stewardship of God's creation? How do we care for the earth and pass a "better world" to the generations yet to come?
4. How can we conserve our limited natural resources? Have we become such "greedy consumers" that we may bring irreversible harm to our environment?
5. Why is Sabbath important? How do you observe Sabbath? Think of creative ways that we could celebrate Sabbath as God intended.

Chapter Two

The Second Creation Story: Adam and Eve, and the Fall

Genesis 2:4—4:17

THE TEXT

When the Lord made the earth and the heavens—and no shrub
of the field had yet appeared on the earth and no plant of the
field had yet sprung up…and there was no man to work the
ground…the Lord formed the man from the dust of the ground
and breathed into his nostrils the breath of life and the man
became a living being. Now the Lord God had planted a
garden in the east, in Eden and there he put the man he had
formed . . . in the middle of the garden were the tree of life
and the tree of the knowledge of good and evil . . . .

—Genesis 2:4-5, 7-9

The Lord God took the man and put him in the Garden of
Eden to work it and take care of it. And the Lord God
commanded the man, "You are free to eat from any tree in
the garden but you must not eat from the tree of the
knowledge of good and evil for when you eat of it you will
surely die. The Lord God said, It is not good for the man to
be alone. I will make him a helper suitable for him . . . ."

—Genesis (2:15-18)

But for Adam no suitable helper was found. So the Lord God caused the man to fall into a deep sleep; and while he was sleeping he took one of the man's ribs . . . then the Lord God made a woman from the rib . . . and he brought her to the man . . . . The man and his wife were both naked and they felt no shame . . .

—Genesis 2:20b-25

"You will not surely die," the serpent said to the woman. For God knows that when you eat of it your eyes will be opened and you will be like God, knowing good and evil . . . . When the woman saw that the fruit of the tree was good for food and pleasing to the eye, and also desirable for gaining wisdom, she took some and ate it. She also gave some to her husband . . . . Then the eyes of both of them were opened and they realized they were naked so they sewed fig leaves together and made coverings for themselves.

—Genesis 3:4, 6-7

And he said, "Who told that you were naked? Have you eaten from the tree that I commanded not to eat from?" The man said, "The woman you put here with me—she gave me some fruit from the tree and I ate it." . . . Then the Lord said to the woman, "What is this you have done?" The woman said, "The serpent deceived me, and I ate." . . . "By the sweat of your brow you will eat your food until you return to the ground, since from it you were taken; for dust you are and to dust you will return . . . .

—Genesis 3:11-13, 19

"Then the Lord said to Cain, "Where is your brother Abel?"

"I don't know," he replied. "Am I my brother's keeper?"

—Genesis 4:9

THE CONTEXT

As the reader can see, in Genesis there are not one, but two creation stories.

The first concludes with 2:4a, **This is the account of the heavens and the earth when they were created**. The second creation story begins with chapter 2:4b: **When the Lord made the earth and the heavens—and no shrub of the field had yet appeared on the earth and plant of the field had yet sprung up, for the Lord God had not sent rain on the earth and there was no man to work the ground...the Lord formed the man from the dust of the ground and breathed into his nostrils the breath of life and the man became a living being.** In this second creation story (Genesis 2: 4b-25), the order of creation is reversed. Man is created first, followed by the trees and animals, and lastly, woman.

The two stories are different. The first is stark in its majestic sweep; the second uses a simple pictorial approach. The wording of the first is precise, but the second is written with less care. They move in different thought-forms. In the first creation story the sexes are created together: **male and female he created them.**(Genesis 1: 27b) In the second version of creation, the Lord creates woman from man: **This is now bone of my bones, flesh of my flesh, she shall be called 'woman' for she was taken out of man.** (Genesis 2:23) In the first creation story, (Genesis 1-2:4), man and woman are created in the image of God. They are separated from the animals and given authority to have dominion over them. The author(s) omits the story of Adam and Eve, the Garden, and the Fall.

11

The writer of the second story has no mechanics of creation. He assumes without description, **God made the heavens and the earth.** (Genesis 2:4b) then expands (2:4b-25) into the creation of man, placing him in a ready-made garden watered by **streams that came up from the earth and watered the whole surface of the ground,** (2:6) In other words, the garden required no work. God then creates woman from the man's rib and instructs the two not to eat of the fruit from the tree in the middle of the Garden. The chapter closes with, **The man and his wife were both naked and they felt no shame.** (2:25)

Despite their differences, the two stories are similar in their common goal: God's crowning creation of humankind and structuring of all else around it. (Genesis 2:4b) As in most creation stories, neither contains a dualistic struggle between opposing forces or two gods vying for control. The will of a single Deity acts. Though they possess different core truths, the two are intricately intertwined. The fundamental truth of the first half of the second creation story, Genesis 2:4-25, echoes the theme of the first creation story. The focus is on God as the sole creator of the universe. Emphasis in the second half, Genesis 3-4:17, is on Adam and Eve in the Garden of Eden, accountability for the presence of evil in the world, and the Fall of humankind. In the second creation story, for example, we see the beginning of the relationship of God to the world, of God to humanity, of humanity to the world, of male to female, and individuals to individuals. A secondary purpose in the second story is to demonstrate the unpleasant consequences which happen to people when they disobey God's laws. The story of Cain and Abel is an outcome and subplot of this latter theme. In the second creation story, therefore, we see the beginning of the relationship of God to the world, of God to humanity, of humanity to the world, of male to female, and individuals to individuals.

The narrative in the second story portrays God's creation of Adam on the same day he created earth and heaven. With this Type-A God, presto, the world is there, no six or seven days. Adam is immediately placed in a garden which God has already planted and will constantly water. Nothing is required of Adam; no effort on his part is needed. He is on welfare or "God-fare" unless he messes up. In Genesis 2:18 God decides to create a companion for Adam which he accomplishes by using one of Adam's ribs (vv 22-24). The command to **not eat from the tree of the knowledge of good and evil, for when you eat of it you will surely die,** (v 17) precedes the creation of woman (vv 22-24).

Though the full presentation of the story begins at 2:4 and ends at 3:23, the invasion of sin and Fall of humanity begins at 3:1 and concludes at 3:23. The episode is unparalleled in the Old Testament and never mentioned again. The participation of Adam and Eve appears balanced: she instigates the act; he participates in the inquiry. According to the late theologian Dietrich Bonhoeffer, "Eve falls first...But the culmination of the story is the fall of Adam. Eve only falls totally when Adam falls...Adam falls because of Eve, Eve falls because of Adam, the two are one."[3]

Evil occurs but the devil is never mentioned. There is good reason: monotheism. There is no devil at this early stage of Jewish religious development. There is only one God and He has no competition. The primary purpose of this second creation story is not to document the origin of evil, but focus on the human response to temptation and the guilt which follows. Humans must claim ownership for their sins. We find no account here of the Fall of Lucifer, as we do in Dante, Milton, and Catholic theology. Bonhoeffer again: "In the entire story the devil incarnate is never introduced."[4] The words sin and repent do not appear.

Woman shows no fear or anxiety in her casual encounter with the snake. Immediately, the snake puts God at the center of the conversation: **Did God really say, "You must not eat from any tree in the garden?"** Throughout the discussion, God remains the focus as the serpent presents possibilities. There is no pressure on the part of the snake. He contradicts God: they will not die. Eve is left with a decision. The tree offers good nutritious food. What is wrong with gaining wisdom from the nutrition? When the fruit is offered to Adam, he does not resist. With no forethought of consequence, he partakes even though he has been warned by God. (2:16). Their eyes are opened; they hide from God. With this transgression of God's will, their perspective changes. Everything looks different. The party is over. The first humans are on their own. They are off God-fare.

Inquest follows the act. God, as judge, conducts a court of inquiry. The balance between male and female is seen again within the context of the dialogue. Woman is the primary dialogue partner with God in 3:1-5 and man serves that role in 3: 9-12. In this more primitive story, God takes on strong personal, anthropomorphic images. He approaches his first humans with physical presence. They hear **the sound of the Lord God as he was walking in the garden in the cool of the day.** (3:8b) They respond with fear and feel naked before their Creator. What happened to make them feel naked? What has this new knowledge done to the first man and woman? These key questions have been debated by theologians for centuries. Both male and female deflect responsibility. They play the blame game. Man blames the woman. Woman blames the serpent. God condemns the serpent first then the couple and addresses the woman before the man. She must endure pain through the labor of childbirth; he must endure pain through toil and sweat. Then comes his ominous final sentence: **"...dust you are and to dust you will return."** "The wages of sin is death." (Romans 6:23) After pronouncing the judgment, God does not abandon them in this garden that has suddenly been turned into a courtroom. He continues in relationship with them. They will need him now in all aspects of their life: their union, children, relationships, work, education, play, ageing. Vanished are bliss, innocence, and harmony. Ever present are sin, guilt and disharmony. It is a new day, a new world.

The story of Cain and Abel has long intrigued interpreters. Many scholars consider the story independent of its current context and setting. It follows as a subplot to the story of Adam and Eve and mirrors the origin of sin into the world through disobedience and revolt to God. With the story of these two sons a dominant theme appears throughout Genesis, the issue of primogeniture or right of the eldest son to inherit.

The writers could have stopped with the story of Adam and Eve and the Fall and jumped forward to Chapter 12 in *Genesis*, the call of Abraham and the beginning of Israelite history. This, however, would have omitted a series of genealogies. Through the Flood and Tower of Babel stories, the genealogies serve as links including Israel in God's world plan. A transitional hinge verse is Genesis 5: 1: **This is the written account of Adam's line**. The author then recapitulates the creation event, reiterating that male and female were created in God's likeness. This is followed by a genealogy from Adam to Noah. Cain and Abel, therefore, serve as a necessary step in a primeval history which serves as a prologue to the central Hebrew epic of Abraham and the Hebrew people.

With the story of Cain, life branches into two different modes of existence: farming and herding. The stories of Cain and Abel in their earliest forms (there were several versions) reflected tensions and conflicts between herdsmen and farmers. Abel, the herder, sacrifices the first born of his flock and is shown favor over Cain, the tiller of the ground. But, this is not the key issue. Central to this story is the cause of family problems after the parents' disobedience to God: This is what happens when you disobey God's will. The father's sin lives on in his son. Like father, the son passes the buck: **Am I my brother's keeper**. (Genesis 4: 9b) A similar dysfunction family theme reoccurs in the stories of Eli and David.

The ground is cursed again with Abel's blood and Cain, a murderer, leaves and builds the first city. (4:17) The first civilization is off to an ominous beginning. What follows is violence, lust, unbridled passion and a chain reaction of evil that runs through the Bible from bad to worse.

THE MESSAGE

Creation

The Bible does not begin at Genesis 12 with the birth of Israel and the call of Abraham, the logical starting point for compiling the history of Israel. It does not begin with the birth of America or Russia or the Peoples Republic of China. It begins with the earth, the whole world. The beginning of the entire Judeo-Christian Bible begins with creation, and not Israel, which has strong implications for contemporary politics and theology.

There are profound implications in this order of creation and history. The God of creation is the God of all people, not just Israel.

This means He is the God of communists, Muslims, gays, criminals, Republicans, Democrats, etc. Israel (the United States?) is actually secondary to the rest of the world. This theme also has implications for the country Israel on the current geopolitical plane. The rest of the world, in the order of creation, comes first. God's creative energy was at work on behalf of all people long before Israel fully understood his redemptive work on its behalf. In other words, when the scribes and historians of Israel finally reach this conclusion, they are catching up with a plan that has been long in place, millennia long.

On a personal level, we as individuals often experience God's redemptive grace and saving acts in our own lives long before we acknowledge his creative acts. This may be symbolically reflected in the New Testament's higher level of popularity among Christians in contrast to the Old Testament. Perhaps our redemptions receive more attention than our creations. The immediacy of God's grace is more easily accepted. Its background and history are more difficult to comprehend. Individuals are not the centerpiece of God's saving works, neither is Israel. God's salvation plan includes all humankind. That concept is difficult for some who feel America is a part of God's real estate and the cross uniquely planted on its soil.

In the New Testament, this universal plan of salvation is reflected in the Gospel of Luke whose genealogy encompasses all humanity, extending all the way back to Adam (3:23-37)[5] and concluding with his prophesy and command to his disciples that "repentance and forgiveness of sins will be preached in his name to *all nations*, beginning at Jerusalem," (24:45, italics the authors.) This theme of universal salvation was further trumpeted by Paul throughout the Mediterranean region. Otherwise, Christianity would have become a Jewish caliphate and died a quiet life in the streets of Jerusalem or the trans-Jordan desert.

The idea of God creating the entire world, inclusive of all individuals and nations, cuts against narrow worldviews and narrow theologies, particularly those that place individual salvation over and above the needs and salvation of other individuals and nations. Luke knew this and makes it clear in his gospel that God's plan of salvation includes everyone.

Against this grand scale of creation, the author of the second creation story zooms in with a dynamic personal touch on the story of Adam and Eve and their offspring Cain and Abel. The author obviously realized something was missing in the first creation story.

God and humanity cannot be fully understood unless seen within the context of their relationship to one another, as well as, how humans relate to humans and how the sexes interact

The emphasis, therefore, shifts from God's creation of the world to his creation of relationships. Regardless of the time frame, this second millennium B.C.E. story of Adam and Eve in the Garden and their offspring comes straight from today's soap operas. Their story is the story of every man and woman and their families. The writer, or writers, who composed and wrote this story, knew it was one for all time.

This story is not about an actual man named Adam and an actual woman named Eve who lived in a place called Eden. Adam and Eve represent the human race, every living person. Their story is the story of every man and woman who live on this earth, the home prepared for them by God. Framed within this context, the stories of Adam and Eve, Cain and Abel, have much to say today.

This story is about *you*.

It is a primitive story filled with dramatic and vivid images. The story of the creation of humankind answers questions that people of all time were probably asking. Why are men and women attracted to each other? Why should people wear clothes? Why do men have to work so hard to provide for their families? Why does a woman have to endure such pain in giving birth? If readers are not careful, they might get lost in the writer's attempt to explain too much and lose the central point. The most important question deals with the relationship of the man and the woman to their creator. The key point is an attempt to account for the presence of evil in the world. The trouble begins when Adam and Eve are tempted to act as though they were equal to God.

The Fall: Bad Choices

The term used most often for the Garden of Eden is "Paradise." Joseph Campbell describes it as "a metaphor for that innocence that is innocent of time, innocent of opposites, and that is the prime center out of which consciousness then becomes aware of the changes."[6] That seems an apt description of the environment and the situation in which Adam and Eve found themselves. It was a time of innocence, absolute dependence, everything they needed for survival and pleasure was handed to them. The fruit was on the vine, the fish were in the sea. God was obviously pleased with what he had created.

What happened to alienate Adam and Eve from the God who created them and called them "good?" What went wrong? That question must have been on the minds of those who told and retold the story through the ages.

First of all, was it a "fall down," as in falling from God's grace, or a "fall up," an attempt to elevate to God's level? The issue is one of dependency versus independency. It could also be an issue about parenting. Does God want us so dependent upon him that we cannot make decisions for ourselves? Or does He encourage independency, exploring, experimenting, and testing? If humans are to become truly "human," do they not need to move from under the umbrella of parental control? In order to become independent must they not make their own decisions, plot their own course? We envision those first beasts of the field and birds of the air lurking from behind and within the first trees and bushes and hear a chorus crying out, "Go, Man, go. Go, Woman, go." After all, does the problem not belong to God? It was He who created the world, the people, the serpent, the scenes. It was He who gave freedom of will to his first people. Should the responsibility not stop with Him? "It is a revolt," claims Bonhoeffer. "It is defection; it is the fall from being held in creatureliness."[7]

Despite the interpretation, humans did "fall out" with their Creator. The words and images tell the story of separation, alienation, and estrangement. In these respects the story not only reflects the past, but also reflects the character of human life and its disharmonious relations in every age and at all levels of life.

People have choices. Sometimes they make wrong choices. The choices people make tend to largely shape their lives. Albert Camus, one of the great existentialists of the twentieth century said, "We become our choices." Stated another way, whatever way we chose to be on earth; that is the way we will be. God did not make his first humans as puppets on a string. Mirroring his own freedom, in his own image, he gave Adam and Eve freedom of will, therefore freedom of choice. He gave them the freedom to choose to disobey. In fact, their first challenge was to listen to God or to listen to the serpent. The serpent might very well be symbolic of that little voice in all of us that sometimes leads us astray.

But where Adam and Eve sinned magnanimously, was in trying to be like God. There were two trees in the garden. One was the tree of life, no prohibitions with it and living a full life. The other was the tree of the knowledge of good and evil. It could also be called the Tree of Being Like God, or the Judgment Tree. From Genesis throughout the Old Testament and into the New Testament, like the theme of a great symphony, "judge not" surfaces over and over. The story of Adam and Eve partaking of the fruit of that particular tree is the story of every neighbor casting judgment on neighbor, every preacher casting aspersions on another denomination or religion, every politician branding their opponent. What does this Old Testament story have to say today? Do not judge.

Accountability: The Blame Game

This story is about more than bad choices. It is the beginning of a key concept which permeates the Bible: spiritual accountability. It is a story about wrong choices, playing the blame game, and defying God's desires for his creation. Adam first blamed God ("**The woman you put here with me...**") then Eve ("**—she gave me some fruit from the tree...**") (3:12). Eve blamed the serpent ("**The serpent deceived me.**") (3:13b) All of them were losers. Adam had to perform back breaking work in the fields to provide for his family. Eve had to suffer the pains of childbirth. The snake had to crawl on his belly for the remainder of his life. Centuries later, we are making the same mistakes. Truly, this ancient story has much to say today.

Some people go through life and never assume responsibility for their own actions. The word responsibility comes from a Latin word, *responder,* which means "to answer for." Many people today have difficulty "answering for," claiming ownership of their faulty, bad decisions. In psychology all of this ties into the theory of attribution. To what do we attribute our failures? To what do we attribute our successes? In psychological jargon, there are two terms to keep in mind: internal locus of control and external locus of control. If students fail a test and blame their failure (the blame game again) on the teacher for an unfair test, distractions in the room, bad luck, or a host of other reasons outside of themselves, they exhibit external locus of control. They attribute their failure to factors outside of themselves. Does this sound like Adam and Eve or anyone else we know?

But if students fail a test and attribute their failure to lack of effort or study, that is an example of internal locus of control. In other words it is called contrition, repentance: "I did it, forgive me." By the same token those same students who make high grades and attribute their high grades to effort and study exhibit internal locus of control. They claim ownership for their success. Often we see students make good grades and call it "luck," a form of external locus of control. They attribute their success to some force or factor outside themselves. Individuals with external locus of control attribute their behaviors, good or bad, to factors outside themselves. They have little sense of identity, of who they are, and of where they are going. They never develop a true sense of self.

To Repent or Not to Repent

We return to Adam and Eve. They are the first, and perennial, blame game players. Is deficit of identity one of the reasons Eve at first has no name? In the story of Adam and Eve there is no contrition, no sense of personal wrong-doing. The words "I am sorry, forgive me," do not appear. The couple is banished from Paradise. We must surely wonder what would have happened if each had said, "Lord, I'm sorry. Please forgive me." Would the cherubim have been removed, the gates of the garden opened, the flaming sword guarding the tree of life extinguished?

Is it not the cherished goal of all of us to get back into the garden and Paradise, return to innocence? Is Paradise not another name for the "kingdom of heaven?" Are they not the same? And how do we gain access? By repenting. The theme repeats itself in the New Testament.—

"Repent, for the kingdom of heaven is near." (Matthew: 4:17) "The kingdom of God is near. Repent and believe the good news." (Mark 1:15) "But unless you repent you too will all perish. (Luke 13:3) "I tell you the truth, unless you change and become like little children, you will never enter the kingdom of heaven." (Matthew 18: 3) Other similar scriptures abound. (Luke 15: 7,10; Luke 17:3; Matthew 7:21). The point is clear that one must obey the Lord and do His will. Obeying the Lord Yahweh is not the strong suit of His first humans. Repentance is not in their behavioral repertoire.

Within that perspective, this may be one Old Testament story that has little to say today. But wait a minute. It is not the only Old Testament story lacking in this area. In the Old Testament, repentance does not improve, not for a while. King David does not repent. He is sorry but he does not repent, which means turning around, going a different direction. In the *King James Version,* the word repent surfaces twice in Genesis chapter six but it is God, no human, who repents. ("And it repented the Lord that he had made man on earth . . . " and " . . . for it repented me that I have made them."(vv.6, 7)[8] Reference to repentance of people in the Bible surfaces in Exodus 13:17: "The people repent when they see war." Even this statement is made by God, not human contrition seeking forgiveness. The pages span many generations and hundreds of years, before the prophets appear where the theme begins to resonate (Jeremiah 15:19, "If you repent, I will restore you.") This is picked up later in the New Testament with John the Baptist and Jesus, both of whom stood in the Old Testament prophetic line.

Stewardship

Consistent with the theme of personal responsibility to God and to each other, is our responsibility to take care of the earth, the garden given to us. The authors of the two creation stories were not in agreement on some issues, but they were in unison about stewardship of the earth. Both writers evoke the directive to be good stewards. Because of its striking and urgent relevance for our time, we pick up the theme again in this second creation story.

The writer's words are clear: **the Lord took the man and put him in the Garden of Eden to work it and take care of it.** (2:15) This reference suggests that God saw Adam (humankind) as an extension of His creative power. One might even paraphrase this verse to read, "I have done my work of creating this paradise, now it is up to you to see that it is cultivated and properly maintained." Also, recall that Adam was created first and put in charge of naming the creatures. Responsibility came early.

The intent with the word "care" implied much more than simply maintaining. In "A Statement of Faith of the United Church of Canada," we affirm, "We are not alone, we believe in God'…" This modern affirmation of faith calls us into partnership with God in God's continuing work of creation. For any religious sect that includes the book of Genesis in its canon, the implications are profound for doctrine as well as practice. No status quo is intended here. There is no return to golden ages or going back and reconstructing time and culture. Humankind must be involved in the ongoing creative process.

In the theories of evolution and creationism, creation moves forward and causes change. Human responsibility must change with it. Denuding the great forests and jungles of the planet, poisoning its air, polluting its waters, or exploiting its natural resources for personal gain are seriously disobedient to God. Do we commit these grievous misdeeds against the earth because we think we created it or own it? Are we declaring ourselves to be "God," so we can do whatever we like? Joseph Campbell explains,

> This we know, the earth does not belong to man,
>
> man belongs to the earth. All things are connected
>
> like the blood that unites us all. Man did not weave
>
> the web of life, he is merely a strand in it. Whatever he
>
> does to the web, he does to himself.[9]

Little things go a long way in our being good stewards of God's good earth. Cleaning up litter in our neighborhoods and on our roadways, planting a garden, recycling, driving slower, turning off unused lights are good stewardship practices that praise God. Saving energy, especially energy from fossil fuels, is one way to help sustain our earth and its atmosphere. By conserving and using renewable sources of energy, we are helping God in the creative process. In the fragile environment where the atmosphere is thinning and the polar caps are melting, it is our God-directed duty—**take care of it.** We must be engaged in the practices that mitigate against conspicuous consumption and waste. Global warming is a reality that has the potential to change our planet in unforeseen and destructive ways if we do not care for the good gift of God's good creation.

Sexuality

The issue of human sexuality has received much attention over the centuries. In the first creation story the author states: **So God created man in his own image, in the image of God he created him: male and female he created them.(1:27)** The approach of the author in the second story differs. Man and woman are created last, after all other creation is in place. It was not good for man to be alone. He needed a helper. Consistent with his older anthropomorphic tendencies this writer goes into graphic detail. Adam falls into a deep sleep and the Lord, in one swift surgical movement, fashions Eve from one of his ribs. This new helper becomes **bone of my bones and flesh of my flesh.** (2:23) Man must leave father and mother (who, at this point, do not exist) and unite with his helper, now called his wife. Like a father of the bride, God leads the man to the woman.

This relationship is the perfect love, unblemished, untainted, without distrust or dishonor. **The man and his wife were both naked, and they felt no shame.** (2:25) Sexual intimacy is uplifted. Man and wife generally do not feel shame when unclothed in the presence of each other. But, there is a literary foreshadowing here. Shame is around the corner. Then comes the Fall and their lives unravel. In the Bible, as in great fiction and great media stories, the main characters tumble from lofty heights. And often, sex plays a major role. This old story once again, speaks today.

Like everything God created—human, animal, and plan—sexuality was considered "good." Maleness and femaleness became a positive part of the created order. The Jewish theologians who admitted "Song of Solomon" into the Hebrew canon must have agreed. The writers and compilers of what we have now as the Old Testament also agreed. Most of Genesis, large segments of the Pentateuch, and the "Monarchy" books (1 and 2 Samuel, 1 and 2 Kings, 1 and 2 Chronicles) are filled with sexual material that is comparable to the "soap opera" of today.

The responsibility of procreation (*pro+creare*=before+creation) is given through the joining of male and female. Conceiving and bearing a child is more than merely a biological function. Properly understood, procreation makes us co-creators with God in the perpetuation of the human race. We insure the image of God *lives* on.

But sex can, and does, turn bad. "Man is creative in destroying," states Bonhoeffer. "In sexuality mankind preserves itself in its destruction. Unrestrained sexuality, like uncreative sexuality, is therefore destruction *par excellence.*"[10] After the Fall, man and woman are divided. Nakedness is an attitude of unity. "Nakedness does not know it is naked."[11] But when the unity is shattered, nakedness becomes shame and must cover itself.

On this theme of sexuality, there is a passage which, if removed from context, would suggest male domination. (3:16b) But, the weight of this second creation story indicates the author was far ahead of his time. The message implies that the relationship between husband and wife was intended by God to be a mutual and approving with love and self-respect. Domination of woman by man is an evil thing. Nowhere does the writer suggest one should dominate the other. The man is to leave his parents and "be united with his wife and they will become one flesh."(2:24) God's rebuke of Adam following verse 3:16 is more harsh than any rebuke to Eve. Bonhoeffer offers a balanced interpretation:

> It is best to describe this unity by saying that now
>
> he belongs to her because she belongs to him. They are no
>
> longer without one another; they are one, and yet two.
>
> The fact of two becoming one is itself the mystery
>
> which God has established by his action upon the

sleeping Adam. They were one from their origin
and only when they become one do they return to
their origin.[12]

Even in their fall they are united. Eve begins the fall. "Eve only falls totally when Adam falls, for the two are one. Adam falls because of Eve, Eve falls because of Adam, the two are one."[13]

Sin

Our tendencies are similar to those of Adam and Eve. We are inclined to follow our own conscience or needs rather than seek God's guidance. The real problem for Adam and Eve seemed to be their desire to run their own lives, in essence, to play God. Against God's wishes, they partook of the fruit of the Tree of the knowledge of Good and Evil and found themselves cast out of Paradise. Going against the commands of God is called sin. Sin is a sure ticket out of the Garden.

Another perspective on sin includes the more popular conception of *"doing something"* wrong against God's wishes, which misses the meaning of the early story. By partaking of the fruit from the tree of the knowledge of good and evil, Adam and Eve gained the knowledge that they were not God and they could never be, or be like, God. This is called being human. It is a state of existence that is also *sin*. In other words, sin is not something we do or a specific transgression, sin is who we are. It is a state of being separated from God. To be human means to be not-God and being not-God is sin. This was the central consistent theme of Jesus of Nazareth: we are *all* sinners. If sin were things we did, or did not do, we could simply keep a checklist. The Pharisees and scribes had a checklist. It was called the Law, the Law of Moses, Deuteronomy, and the Prophets, the same handed down over the generations. But the Law could never make one right, or righteous, or saved because no one could meet all of the demands of the Law. This is where God's grace comes into the picture, the "good news" Jesus preached. The gospel is that God's grace comes to us in spite of our human entrapment.

Death

…until you return to the ground, since from it you were taken; for dust you are and to dust you will return. (3:19b)

At this point in the story, the German theologian Gerhard von Radd provides a summary:

> …by wanting to be like God, man stepped out
>
> from the simplicity of obedience to God. He
>
> thereby forfeited life in the pleasant garden and
>
> close to God. What remained to him was a life of
>
> toil in the midst of the wearying mysteries involved
>
> in a hopeless struggle with the power of evil, and,
>
> at the end, to be, without reprieve, the victim of death.[14]

The Tree of Life was within the grasp of Adam and Eve but God cut them off.(3:22) The Tree of Life is still there. It exists as a possibility. This hope is evidenced in the next passage: **Adam named his wife Eve, because she would become the mother of all the living.** (3:20) This is the first reference to *mother* in the Bible. Death, as part of our mortality, is announced. But through Eve and her lineage, life will continue. In his Nobel acceptance speech author William Faulkner proclaimed, "I believe that man will not only endure he will prevail," and goes on to say, "He is immortal, not because he alone among creatures has an inexhaustible voice, but because he has a soul, a spirit capable of compassion and sacrifice and endurance."

The Tree of Life theme surfaces again in the New Testament. God opens the way again to the Tree of Life and shows that redemption is possible. Though Paul takes the theme that sin leads to death but death is overcome through Christ beyond the limits of the story, he accurately interprets the significance of the death of Adam in comparison with the death and resurrection of Christ (5:12-21): "So that just as sin reigned in death, so also grace might reign through righteousness to bring eternal life through Jesus Christ our Lord." (Romans 5: 21)

A Dysfunctional Family

Eve lives up to her name and promise to **become the mother of all the living** (3:20b) and **with the help of the Lord** (4:1b) gives birth to Cain, and later to Abel. Thus, from the perspective of the biblical writers, the generations of humankind were launched. It was not a very promising or auspicious beginning. "Cain is the first man to be born upon the cursed ground. The whole story of death begins with Cain."[15]

Within a short time, (the scripture states **in the course of time—4:3**) there is conflict. Emotions and behavior move from one extreme to the other; from evoking God's name to lying to him, from intimacy to jealousy, from harmony to violence. The writers seem to say, "This is what happens when people disobey God."

The God who created this situation, to some degree, stays out of the mix. God does not intervene. Cain must make his own decision, decide one way or another with the knowledge God has given to him. Cain should not catastrophize. God wills that we learn from our mistakes and move forward.

The blame game is passed on. Abel is blamed for something he did not do, which leads to his death. Did God, through his own actions, lead to Abel's death? Is this perhaps one of the reasons Cain receives a lighter sentence from God? Some commentators say God accepted the responsibility and, in turn, protected the life of Cain. There are other instances in scripture with Moses, Abraham, and ultimately Calvary, where the final responsibility was with God. The link between Christ and Abel is found in Hebrews 12:24—"So Jesus the mediator of a new covenant, and to the sprinkled blood that speaks a better word than the blood of Abel."

The murder of Abel is the first death recorded in the Bible, the first encountered by the new family. No one had ever witnessed death. We wonder how long Cain stood there waiting for his brother to arise. There is also no indication in the text that Cain "intended" to kill Abel. Cain strikes Abel in a moment of anger, a reflex. Ironically, the act was committed during an act of worship. Perhaps Cain's thoughts at the time were focused more on his own shortcomings than on who or what Abel was. Following the deed, Cain cannot avoid God. His conscience cannot hide from the Almighty Creator: **"Where is your brother…?"** (Genesis 4:9) is the question for all humankind. It haunts us day and night. The words echo in Psalms ("Oh Lord you have searched me and you know me…Where can I go from your Spirit?"— 139:1,7) Jonah would discover this later in the Bible. The Psalmist's words reverberate in Francis Thompson's "Hound of Heaven:"

> I fled him down the nights and down the days;
>
> I fled him down the arches of the years;
>
> I fled him down the labyrinthine ways
>
> Of my mind; and in the midst of tears
>
> I hid from Him…[16]

We cannot avoid God.

Cain's parents have been driven from their home. He is expelled from the only home he has known and is doomed to be "a restless wanderer on the earth." (4:14b) Sin has its consequences. The story of this dysfunctional family speaks today.

Bonhoeffer reminds us that "death stands under the mark of Cain. Christ on the Cross, the murdered Son of God, is the end of the story of Cain, and thus the actual end of the story."[17] Paradoxically, paradise, exited under the threat and promise of death, is reentered by death.

The First Urbanizer

The first recording of a city in the Bible is Genesis 4:17 ("Cain was then building a city.") where Cain is depicted as being the originator of urban civilization. He named the city for his son Enoch. Though Cain may not have actually built the city, city-life became a reality over against the nomads who preceded it. Verse 20 suggests civilization began with **those who live in tents and raise livestock.** The early chapters of Genesis portray a close relationship between the people and the land, as though from this intimacy comes both the moral and universal order. By building a city, Cain breaks the pattern and interrupts the rhythm of life. He is a progressive innovator and entrepreneur. Thomas Jefferson, one of this country's Founding Fathers, compared Alexander Hamilton to Cain, as one who represented commerce, technology, stock jobbers, marketing, expansion. In Jefferson's eyes, Hamilton personified the city.

A Concluding Note

The aim of most religions is to re-enter that timeless garden of bliss and innocence. The theme and metaphors of the Genesis story resurfaces in the New Testament where a garden of mental anguish leads to another of eternal bliss. A tree of total suffering and humility replaces another of total pride. These linguistic transitions do not correspond to human logic and reason. Perhaps the writers of both testaments knew this and used the language of story, of metaphor, the language of faith. Perhaps that is why, when all is said and done, we are left wanting more, another sentence in our logic to bring closure. We thank those writers for being true to the language of faith. They teach us to believe…not to know.

> We have but faith: we cannot know;
>
> For knowledge is of things we see;
>
> And yet we trust it comes from thee,
>
> A beam in darkness: let it grow.[18]

Only with imagination, one can draw symbolic parallels between the Garden of Eden and the Garden of Gethsemane,[19] between a tree which brought humankind down and one of crucifixion which, paradoxically, gave it hope. Bonhoeffer capitalizes on the images:

What a strange paradise is this hill of Golgotha, this Cross, this blood, this broke body. What a strange tree of life, this tree on which God himself must suffer and die but it is in fact the Kingdom of Life...The tree of life, the Cross of Christ, the middle of the fallen and preserved world of God, for us that is the end of the story of paradise.[20]

QUESTIONS FOR FURTHER STUDY AND DISCUSSION

1. After reading about both creation stories, brainstorm and list the differences between the two creation stories.
   - Had you been previously aware there were two stories of Creation? If so, what did you learn from this study that was new?
   - Why were there different orders of creation?
   - What does it mean to be created in the image of God? What are the implications of your understanding for the various levels of society: individual, family, community, state, nation?
2. What is sin? The word occurs for the first time at Genesis 4:7.
   - Is there a difference between knowing good and evil and knowing the difference between good and evil?
   - Is knowing the difference and acting accordingly what God expects of us?
   - What does God expect of us?
3. What is evil? Is it the same as sin?
4. Does Satan exist? If so, how is he manifested? Is he responsible for sin?
5. If you believe there is a force known as Satan, how do you reconcile that belief with monotheism, the belief in one God? Do you see a contradiction?
6. Where do you see the "blame game" in your life? Your community? The nation? The world?
7. Based on what you have learned so far in Genesis, what implications, if any, do you see for our current geo-political situation in the mid-East?
8. What would it be like to possess God-like knowledge?
9. Did God through his own actions lead to Abel's death?
   What parallels can you draw between the second creation story and the life of Jesus of Nazareth?

Chapter Three

Noah and the Flood

Genesis 5:28—9:29

THE TEXT:

When Lamech had lived 182 years, he had a son. He named
him Noah and said, "he will comfort us in the labor and
painful toil of our hands caused by the ground the Lord has
cursed , , , After Noah was 500 years old he became the
father of Shem, Ham and Japheth , , ,

—Genesis 5:28-32

The Lord saw how great man's wickedness on the earth had
become, and that every inclination of the thoughts was only
evil all the time . . . So the Lord said, "I will wipe mankind
whom I have created, from the face of the earth—men and
animals and creatures that move along the ground, and birds
of the air—for I am grieved that I have made them. But
Noah found favor in the eyes of the Lord . . .

—Genesis 6:5-8

So God said to Noah, "I am going to put an end to all people,
for the earth is filled with violence because of them . . . . So
make yourself an ark of cypress wood . . . I am going to
bring floodwaters on the earth to destroy all life under the

heavens, every creature that has the breath of life in it. Everything on earth will perish. But I will establish my covenant with you...You are to bring into the ark two of all living creatures, male and female . . . . Noah did everything just as the Lord commanded him . . .

—Genesis 6:13-14, 17-22

Noah was six hundred years old when the floodwaters came on the earth . . . rain fell on the earth for forty days and forty nights . . . . For forty days the flood kept coming on the earth. The waters rose and increased greatly on the earth . . . the waters flooded the earth for a hundred and fifty days. But God remembered Noah . . . . After forty days Noah opened the window he had made in the ark and sent out a raven, and it kept flying back and forth until the water had dried up from the earth. Then he sent out a dove to see if the water had receded from the surface of the ground. But the dove . . . returned. He waited seven more days and again sent out the dove from the ark. When the dove returned to him in the evening, there in its beak was a freshly plucked olive leaf.

—Genesis 7:6, 17; 8:1, 6-12

Then the Lord said to Noah, "Come out of the ark . . . . So Noah came out, together with his sons and his wife and his sons' wives . . . . Then Noah built an altar to the Lord . . . he sacrificed burnt offerings . . . . The Lord smelled the pleasing aroma and said in his heart: "Never again will I curse the ground because of man."

—Genesis 8:15, 21

Then God blessed Noah and his sons, saying to them, "Be fruitful and increase in number and fill the earth." . . . Then God said to Noah and to his sons with him, "I now establish my covenant with you and with your descendants after you and with every living creature that was with you . . . . Never again will all life be cut off by the waters of a flood, never again will there be a flood to destroy the earth . . . . I have set my rainbow in the clouds and it will be the sign of the covenant between me and the earth."

—Genesis 9:1, 8, 13

The Context

Some commentators begin the story of the Flood at Genesis 6:9 with the references to Noah's "account" and the genealogical data of his three sons, yet others contend the Flood story begins at 6:5 with 6:5-8 as a form of prologue. Because of our emphasis upon context and background, we chose to begin the story at Genesis 5:28 with the first mention of Noah and his father.

Was there a flood that destroyed the earth? This is one of the first questions readers often ask themselves. A number of different flood stories circulated throughout the Near East in that time period, and Israel was surely aware of them. The *Gilgamish Epic* was the most widely known. Geological history and research point to the Tigris-Euphrates river valley which was inundated by frequent flooding and was the probable source of these stories. The Black Sea may have been created by a massive flood when a narrow land bridge across the

Bosporus Straight broke and waters from the Mediterranean rushed into the low-lying basin.

Though there is geological evidence for a cataclysmic flood in that region, the key question is not whether the event occurred, but how the story became part of the Bible. What does this flood story have to do with the history and religious faith of Israel? More importantly, what does the story have to say today?

A major thrust of the Flood story was God's control. His established order had been transgressed. Humankind had become increasingly sinful before God. Punishment was in order and punishment is introduced with the story of Noah and the Flood.

Sources indicate the name Noah implied one who would "cause us to settle down."[21] According to biblical genealogy, Noah was the grandson of Methuselah and the ninth descendant from Adam through Seth. God became angry with humans over their immoral behavior and their treatment of the good world He had created. He would start over. Noah, the most righteous man of his time, and his family were chosen to perpetuate the human race.

Like the story of creation, there are two flood stories. According to the account of one ancient author, who we will label P, God commanded Noah to build an ark and collect two of all species. (6:19-20) According to another account by a writer we will call J, God commanded Noah to collect seven (7) pairs of all species.(7:2-4) Then it rained for forty days and forty nights (7:11-23) and the ark was afloat for ten months before landing on Mount Ararat. A raven and a dove were sent to survey the area. Only the dove succeeded.. Sacrifices were performed and God promised Noah He would send no more floods. This new covenant was symbolized by a rainbow in the sky. Noah proceeded to plant a vineyard. a story many scholars feel is unrelated to the flood story. As the waters receded, Noah straddled the fence between farming and herding, an echo of the Cain and Abel episode.

The key theme is not the flood as a natural event, but God's judgment in the affairs of history. God acts to establish His righteous purpose. Consistent with His clothing of Adam and Eve after their judgment, and His protection of Cain following his disobedience, God shows concern for humanity. The two stories which follow the Flood episode, Noah's drunken bout and the Tower of Babel, demonstrate that the world is radically infected with evil that no Flood can cure.

THE MESSAGE

At first glance, it might seem that the Flood story in Genesis has very little theological significance for our modern world. Some might even think that the only relevance for today would be the belief that the world depends upon God for its very existence and that humankind is subject to God's justice and judgment. There is definitely more to be gleaned from this ancient story than meets the eye. The meaning of the great story is not dependent upon facts of history. Truth is found in the story.

Be Prepared

Floods are often in the news. In recent years, they have devastated parts of Bangladesh, China, India, Myanmar, and our country. When these deluges occur they are catastrophic. The devastating hurricane Katrina, that flooded the ninth ward of New Orleans and other parts of that city in 2005 causing death and destruction, must have seemed like Noah's Flood to those affected. After the fact, we learned much of the damage could have been prevented with stronger levies. We cannot prevent hurricanes, earthquakes, tornados, or volcanoes, but we can be proactive like Noah. Imagine the ridicule Noah and his sons must have endured when they began to build their Ark on dry ground, with no cloud in sight. Their neighbors and friends must have thought Noah and his family had "lost it." The building of the Ark must have been considered the height of folly to those observing its construction. Noah could see things they could not see. One is reminded of Jesus' comment, "You know how to interpret the appearance of the sky but you cannot interpret the signs of the times." (Matthew 16:3) A modern parallel might be those in the 60's building bomb shelters when the atom threat was real.

God calls us to be prepared. We can prepare and take steps to limit the damage. We can plan more carefully. Our civil authorities can establish building codes, strengthen levies, develop and publish evacuation procedures. All of the above would significantly reduce loss of life and property damage. In his parables of "The Wise and Foolish Virgins" (Matthew 25:1-13) and "The Wise and Foolish builder" (Matthew 7:24-28), Jesus used a different metaphor but delivered the same message: Be prepared. In the story of the virgins, those who used all their oil could not light their lamps when "the bridegroom came." They missed the wedding festivities. With the Foolish Builder, when the winds and rain came, his house would not stand. It was not built on a firm foundation.

Ecological Implications

There are significant ecological implications in the story of Noah and the Flood. Some experts contend flooding around the world is increasing because of changes in weather patterns caused by global warming. Global warming, which began early in the twentieth century, is the increase in the earth's average surface and ocean temperature. Most respected scientific organizations agree this phenomenon is caused by the over-use of fossil fuels such as coal and oil. In other words, this global problem is being brought on by human excess and irresponsibility. Scientific evidence suggests the massive, catastrophic floods of our time are being caused by pollution due to human waste and irresponsibility. In the story in Genesis, the Flood results from humans polluting the earth with misdeeds and sinful behavior. Are the truths of biblical stories repeating today? Is this what the story of Noah and the Flood say today?

The long term results of our ecological misdeeds could be devastating. One of the results of global warming is the loss of great glaciers that will eventually raise the sea level and cause massive flooding in coastal areas. The rise in temperature, caused by fossil fuels and other pollutants, will become a greater threat to the habitats that sustain much of animal life. In addition to the threat to animal life, the potential rise in the sea level will threaten coastal areas around the world. For example, Florida would become submerged. No one can predict all the consequences of global warming but future generations could be catastrophically affected.

The problems noted above are caused by human behavior. Human behavior in the early Genesis chapters led to expulsion from the Garden. The sins of the generations grew exponentially until they reached universal proportions. Is this happening today with our sins against the natural cosmic order? Most would agree we are being reminded of the close relationship between moral and cosmic order. When we disobey one, we reap the consequences of the other. God does not send the punishment. The punishment is built into the natural order he created. One might say God's judgment was "hard-wired" at creation. By committing the sins against the natural order, we draw the punishment upon ourselves. It is *quid pro quo.* This aspect of the Flood story is not myth. It is awesome, eye-opening, reality. Are we, through our exploitation of God's creation, bringing on a second flood?

Starting Over

The story of the Flood is about cleansing and starting over. God's humanness, personified centuries later in Jesus the Christ, is manifested in his anger and frustration with humankind. Like some perfectionists (psychologists refer to the phenomenon as OCD—Obsessive Compulsive Disorder), God pitches a fit. His creation will be all or nothing. Then he cools down, re-evaluates, and decides there are aspects of humanity that are salvageable and he keys on Noah, a "righteous man." Jesus' outburst when he cleansed the Temple might be seen as a parallel to God's outburst and cleansing of the world with the flood. Some writers also draw comparisons with the Flood and baptism.

Saving the Animals

All life is precious to God. That animals were saved along with Noah and his family is an indication that the early Hebrews believed all life was sacred and worth saving.

"Positively, it is striking that God puts such stock in the saving of animals, indeed, God's remembrance of the animals belongs to the same initiative as God's remembering Noah. The lives of animals and humans are so interconnected that our future on this planet is limited to one another's well-being."[22]

Since animals are important to our life on this planet, the preservation of animal life is a sacred calling to all of us who inhabit this limited sphere. An ecological concern for saving endangered species is more than a political issue, it is an issue of "the stewardship of the earth" and of all the animals given by God to the first humans. The key word is balance. The earth is sustained by ecological balance. Ecological balance is a state of equilibrium in which the human, animal, and other organisms depend on each other for stability and existence.

We depend upon animals, fish, and insects, for our existence. When ecosystems are thrown out of balance, the existence of the organisms within that system is threatened. In this perspective, the truth from the story of the Flood becomes clear. Noah saved humanity and animals from extinction.

The growing problem of animal cruelty is an important concern. Through experimentation, factory farming, the fur trade, hunting, and entertainment billions of animals die each year. Staggering statistics reveal that annually over 70 million animals are tortured and killed in U. S. laboratories. More than 10 billion are slaughtered for human consumption and twenty percent of laying hens die of stress-related diseases in cramped quarters (four or five confined to a 14 inch cage). The fur trade industry is responsible for the deaths of over 35 million fur-bearing animals each year, most of those killed by trapping. Over 2.7 million are harvested on fur farms. Elephants, tigers, rhinos and other endangered species are killed each year by poachers for products sold on the black market. The over-harvesting of fish in the oceans and seas and the slaughter of over a half million seals threaten the eco-balance.

The loss of animal life in the entertainment industry is beyond comprehension. Bullfights claim the lives of over 40 thousand bulls each year in one of the bloodiest, tortuous methods known. Restricted to the confines of marinas and sea zoos, the lives of whales and dolphins are reduced to 25 percent of their natural life. Annually, over 50,000 greyhounds are killed or sent to laboratories when they can no longer compete.[23] Cockfighting has long been outlawed in most parts of this country and more recently dog fighting has come under scrutiny.

The above information represents only a sampling of the facts, validating recent outcries at the degradation and treatment of helpless animals by unkind treatment or harmful practices. To say Noah committed animal abuse by confining the species he gathered into cramped quarters misses the point of the story. God could have told Noah to save only his family. But the scripture clearly states who and what were to be saved: **all living creatures, male and female…every kind of food that is to be eaten (6:19, 21).** Infinite Wisdom was at work here. For God to have ordered Noah to save himself and his family would have required less effort and sacrifice, but a remnant of *all* creation was to be saved.

Noah, Jesus and the Eschaton

There are several elements of the story that remind us of Jesus and his message. The story of Noah and the Flood is apocalyptical, the first in the Bible about eschatology which is the theology of the end of time or eschaton, the last day. Jesus lived in a time of eschatological expectation. He spoke of God's judgment on the last day and the need to be prepared because it would come "like a thief in the night" (1Thessalonians 5:2). Noah saved a remnant and Jesus preached a remnant would be saved. Water became prominent and symbolical in the lives of both men. Both had to contend with turbulent and stormy water, a common theme in the Bible. (Exodus 14-15; Isaiah 43:2 and 8:7-8; Jonah; Matthew 4:335-41; 1 Peter 3:18-22). New Testament references to Noah include the following: Matthew 24:27-28; Luke

3:36; Hebrews 11:7. In 1 Peter 3: 20-21, the deliverance of Noah from the deluge is comparable to deliverance from sin through Christian baptism.

In the story of Noah and the Flood, God's judgment against the sinfulness of humankind did not result in "total destruction." A remnant was saved. The concept of a "righteous remnant" runs throughout the Old Testament. God's salvation of a righteous remnant is a recurring theme for the People of Israel and exemplified in such notables as Abraham, Joseph and Moses. God saves a "remnant" during the Babylonian captivity. Christians believe that a remnant of God's people was saved through the death, and resurrection of Jesus Christ, which takes us to our final point in this chapter.

The Rainbow

The story of the Flood ends on a positive note reflected by the rainbow. God **puts a bow in the sky** to remind Noah and his descendants of a covenant that God is making with humankind: the earth will never again be destroyed with water. This covenant with Noah was to last **as long as the earth endures**.

God is a covenant-making and covenant-keeping God. The Hebrew people came to rely on such assurances from their God. They became known as "God's covenant people." The word "testament" could also be translated "covenant." Therefore, the Old Testament is sacred writing that reassures the people of Israel that they are in a covenant relationship with their Creator-God. Christians are a people of a "New Covenant" with God through Jesus Christ. The cross has become for the New Testament what the rainbow became for the Old Testament, a symbol of hope and of God's promise.

QUESTIONS FOR FURTHER STUDY AND DISCUSSION

1. One of the lessons of the story of the Flood is about starting over. Can you think of current metaphors which exemplify this ability? Reflect on your own life and family where you have seen this happen. Make a list of these metaphors, how they mirror the story of the Flood and how they relate to you in this century.

2. What are the effects of global warming on contemporary life?
   a. How does global warming affect me personally where I live?
   b. What specific steps could I take to be more proactive and help diminish the effects of global warming?

3. By exploiting the natural resources around us are we bringing on a second global catastrophe?

4. Noah's preparedness has implications for all areas of life in which we need to be prepared to live successfully. It pays to be prepared for every type of eventuality. A few of those areas include marriage, parenthood, retirement, death. Discuss the ways you can be prepared in each of these.

5. What does this ancient covenant have to do with contemporary life and values? Are we also bound by this covenantal relationship?

Chapter Four

Tower of Babel

THE TEXT

Now the whole world had one language and a common speech. As men moved eastward, they found a plain in Shinar and settled there.

They said to each other, "Come, let's make bricks and bake them thoroughly. They used brick instead of stone, and tar for mortar. Then they said, "Come, let us build ourselves a city, with a tower that reaches to the heavens, so that we may make a name for ourselves and not be scattered over the face of the whole earth."

But the Lord came down to see the city and the tower that the men were building. The Lord said, "If as one people speaking the same language they have begun to do this, then nothing they plan to do will be impossible for them. Come, let us go down and confuse their language so they will not understand each other.

So the Lord scattered them from there over the earth, and they stopped building the city. That is why it was called Babel—because there the Lord confused the language of the whole world. From there the Lord scattered them over the face of the whole earth.

THE CONTEXT

The Tower of Babel[24] story follows the peopling of the earth by Noah's three sons (Shem, Ham, and Japheth) and ends the primeval history of the Bible: Creation, Adam and Eve, Cain and Able, and the Flood. According to Old Testament authority Gerhard von Radd, "The story of the Tower of Babel is therefore to be regarded as the end of the road upon which Israel stepped out with the Fall, and which led to more and more serious outbreaks of sin."[25] Other scholars believe the story is a compilation of another writer we have called J as an introduction to his story of Abraham and the beginning of the history of Israel which would account for the origin of Israel as one of the different people on the earth.[26]

Unlike the stories of the Creation and the Flood, the Tower of Babel episode stands alone in Mid-Eastern lore.[27] Some parallels exist but the story is endemic to Hebrew history and culture. It has an affinity with the Flood story in that one theme is the separation of God and humanity. The Tower story is also an answer to the age old question: How did it happen there are many languages and people cannot understand each other?

The story is also based, in part, on historical fact which leads to another theme: the collision of the Hebrew faith and their God with the religions surrounding them. Tribes and ethnic groups from the steppes bordering the Fertile Crescent continuously migrated into the Tigris-Euphrates valley and eastward across the Crescent into Palestine. Nomadic Semites, who would later comprise the nations of Israel and Judah, included some of these tribes. According to one theory, the inhabitants of the Tigris-Euphrates plain built towers as sanctuaries of worship which served as altars nearer to the sky or heaven. Enter the Hebrews and their God and the beginning of a long continuous struggle against the worship of alien gods. In the Tower of Babel story, the writer condemns the worship of foreign deities but also denounces the presumption of human design without consulting God's will. This leads to their downfall and further separation from God which is sin. God's judgment scatters the tower builders, which creates different languages.

The Tower of Babel story is a short story with a typical short story plot: character, event, change. In this case, the character is not an individual but **the whole world**. The event is God's intervention ("God came down"). Change is the leveling of a national pride and scattering of its people.

The narration is divided into two distinct parts: verses 1-4 describe the materials and plan of the tower construction; verses 5-9 report the counter-plans of the Deity. The passage turns on verse 5, the judicial inquest: **But the Lord came down.** The scene is set in Shinar

(Babylonia). To achieve and maintain unity, the people decide to build a city and a tower that would reach to the heavens. From the point of view of the author, the incident that was originally designed to create recognition and a name turned into an act of arrogance and a revolt against God. The human spirit of that culture had become corrupted by pride and its counterpart greed. Similar to the Flood story, God intervened and created confusion in their ability to communicate, which halted the construction and scattered them over the face of the earth. The story evokes the question of God's relationship to the nations. Was it totally ruptured? Did God exhaust his grace with the people of the world? The Tower of Babel story concludes the primeval prologue (Genesis 1-10) and sets up the saga of Abraham that serves as a bridge to the ancient writer's original purpose, the saving history of Israel.

THE MESSAGE

The Tower of Babel story might appear to have nothing to say today. But these nine verses are packed with truth and relevancy for any people in any era. Each phrase resonates with moral message and caution. Readers who pass over this story in favor of more "interesting" stories miss a literary package compressed with spiritual power.

Pride versus Humility

The opening chapters of Genesis began by answering questions: How was the earth created? Who made humans? Why are there male and female sexes? If creation was "good," who, or what, caused it to turn evil? What is the source of evil? With chapter 11 another question arises: Why are there different races with different languages? Why do people have trouble understanding each other?[28]

The profound truths and insights behind the Tower of Babel story, carefully woven into its texture, are as relevant today as they were then. This is a story about trouble in the world and human history, a story about what happens when pride oversteps its boundaries. "Pride goes before destruction, a haughty spirit before a fall" (Proverbs

16::18). Millennia later Shakespeare echoed similar thoughts: "He that is proud eats up himself. Pride is his own glass, his own trumpet, his own chronicle; and whatever praises itself but in the deed, devours the deed in the praise."[29]

Let us build ourselves a city, with a tower that reaches to the heavens. (11:4) With a few quick strokes of his quill, the ancient writer encapsulates human history and the rise of civilizations. In preceding sentences, he portrays a people who are attempting to reach the pinnacle of power through their own ingenuity, device and contrivance. The writer was possibly aware of the great Hanging Gardens of King Nebuchadnezzar, allegedly constructed near the Tower of Babel. The wandering Hebrew nomads may have known about the pyramids of the pharaohs or the other gigantic monuments and obelisks erected by thousands of slaves to memorialize a ruler, inscribe his honors and chisel his name on their pedestals.

Let us build ourselves a city with a tower that reaches to the heavens. Others sought a similar eminence: Assyria, Babylon, Persia, Rome. In the pride of power they all sought to build something bigger and greater. Whatever authority had preceded them, including the throne of God, they meant to top it. In our own recent times we have witnessed similar efforts: The Third Reich, The Russia of Lenin and Stalin, Kim Jung Il of North Korea, Saddam Hussein. Would capitalism and the United States of America be included in this list?

Let us build ourselves a city with a tower that reaches to the heavens. The Tower of Babel was the first skyscraper. Twin Towers, Chicago World Trade Center and Empire State Building could be viewed as modern Towers of Babel. Critics decry the greed and exploitation that built them and may well ask, "Is there not in all of these an element of the same blind pride of power which became obsessed with building the tower that ultimately must be confounded?"[30]

Let us build ourselves a city with a tower that reaches to the heavens. And where are the monuments of old now? The answer is found in the second creation story in Genesis, and the judgment of the Lord upon Adam for his pride which led to his misdeeds. **For dust**

you are and to dust you will return. (3:19b) Millennia later, "The cloud-capp'd towers...dissolve."[31]

The Tower no longer exists in reality but its symbolic presence is strong. Humility is the theme of the story. No one nation stands out. There are no chosen people in this story. Humanity is leveled into a swirling mass of confused languages. In the end, the great Tower was never completed. It remained only a stump of envisioned greatness signifying nothing.

> Look on my works, ye mighty, and despair!
>
> Nothing beside remains. Round the decay
>
> Of that colossal wreck, boundless and bare
>
> The lone and level sands stretch away.[32]

Writing centuries later and invested with the power of the Holy Spirit, St. Paul wrote, "If I speak in the tongues of men and of angels, but have not love, I am only a resounding gong or a clanging cymbal...I am nothing." (1 Corinthians 13:1, 2b) Are we hearing those words?

> "Where the temple stood will rise a new building;
>
> the terrible tower of Babel will be built again. And
>
> though, like the one of old, it will not be finished, yet
>
> Thou mightest have prevented that new tower and have
>
> cut short the sufferings of men for a thousand years; for
>
> they will come back to us after a thousand years of agony
>
> with the tower."[33]

Towers continue to rise and fall, symbols of our pride and arrogance, our desires to **make a name** for ourselves. Towers and walls are sources of trouble, suspicion and hostility. Individual, corporate, and national drives to "get to the top" alienate others, cause distrust and miscommunication: "They do not speak our language."

This ancient story teaches us to live with diversity, which includes facing and accepting the language barriers of contemporary life. The perfect world, as depicted by the Tower of Babel, cannot be created by human effort. Building the Kingdom of God, we are servants to a higher power. By submitting to God's lordship we build communities that overcome language and cultural barriers. What happened in that plain in Shinar would be long remembered and resurrected centuries later in Jerusalem. The metaphors are also visible today in our contemporary world.

Babel and Pentecost

As previously noted, the action of the tower builders was oppositional to the divine command to replenish the earth.(Genesis 1:28 and 9:1) The motivation fueling their construction was the fear of being **scattered over the face of the whole earth**. The tower project constituted,

> a bid to secure their own future as a unified
>
> community, isolated from the rest of the world...
>
> their resistance to being scattered (this word
>
> occurs positively in 10:18; cf. 9:19; 10:5, 32)
>
> occasions a divine concern for the very created
>
> order of things, for only by spreading abroad can
>
> human beings fulfill their charge to be caretakers
>
> of the earth.[34]

This theme is reflected at Pentecost. If the disciples remained in Jerusalem, the gospel would not spread. And there was a tremendous temptation on the part of the disciples to keep this fresh new spirit to themselves. Had that happened, Christianity might not have survived. The early church would have become a Jerusalem caliphate with James the brother of Jesus the first caliph and his successors determined by blood lineage. Thankfully, Paul had other ideas.

What occurred at Pentecost, though with a different twist, is a repeat of Babel:

> They were all together in one place. Suddenly a sound
>
> like the blowing of a violent wind came from heaven
>
> and filled the whole house where they were sitting.
>
> They saw what seemed to be tongues of fire that separated
>
> and came to rest on each of them. All of them were filled
>
> with the Holy Spirit and began to speak in other tongues,
>
> as the Spirit enabled them."
>
> —Acts 2:1-4

The remaining narrative indicates, "Jews from every nation under heaven"(2:5) were in the vicinity and upon hearing their own language in amazement asked, "Are not all these men who are speaking Galileans?" These foreign Jews—from Parthia, Mede, Elam, Cappadocia, Asia, Pontus, Phrygia, Egypt, and Rome—heard the Galileans, "declaring the wonders of God in our own tongues."(2:11) Multiple languages erupt yet they all hear and receive the gospel. The myriad tongues do not obscure the hearing of the message. In fact, it is in the diversity of their languages that people are able to hear and comprehend.

Later, in Acts 8, "the apostles were scattered throughout Judea and Samaria." (v.1) The scattering of one nation at Babel is repeated in the scattering of one group of eleven disciples. Pentecost became the new Babel, the place where they spoke in many tongues. Pentecost trumped Babel. At Babel the languages were confused and the people could not understand each other, but at Pentecost the message was understood by all who heard it. At Babel there was a scattering of people who could not communicate. At Pentecost there was a scattering of people because they communicated a gospel of salvation. Pentecost opened a new chapter of the story. One gospel was spoken in many tongues.

Communication is a key theme in the Tower of Babel story. Those who speak different languages and dialects are viewed with skepticism. Even accents can create stereotype perceptions and create communication barriers. The inability to understand the languages of others hinders relationship building. The Babels of our time—the towers of superiority, condescension, arrogance, and elitism—are legion. To eradicate the towers, languages need to be infused with the same single message heard in different tongues at Pentecost: repent for the kingdom of God is at hand.

Self-Preservation versus Universal Concern

The first four verses of the story suggest an isolationist viewpoint which would place the ongoing creative process in jeopardy. God comes down and promotes diversity at the expense of unity that would preserve itself in selfish isolation from the rest of the world.

The scripture states, **Now the world had one language and a common speech,** (11:1), but, in fact, this was a time of great migrations through the mid-East with a flux of many languages. Were the people of Babel threatened by these many different voices and cultures? Did they need to withdraw and insulate themselves to prevent becoming fragmented and forced to wander the earth? This is a possible conclusion that is being fulfilled today. Jews are building walls in Palestine. Americans are building walls along their southern border. Do walls promote peace and brotherly love or do they sow seeds of resentment, suspicion, fear, hostility, and alienation? "Something there is that doesn't love a wall…"[35]

Great civilizations have resulted from great migrations. The United States was a result of waves of immigrants. Our Statue of Liberty symbolizes our open door policy:

> Give me your tired, your poor,
>
> Your huddled masses yearning to breathe free,
>
> The wretched refuse of your teeming shore,
>
> Send these, the homeless, temptest-tossed to me,
>
> I lift my lamp beside the golden door.

This remarkable policy of openness stands in sharp contrast to the closed door of the Tower of Babel, ironically called the "gate of God." From millennia ago, the problems of humanity are unchanged. With amazing freshness, the story of the Tower of Babel speaks to us today. Do we close our doors and by doing so live forever unified in solidarity? Or do we continue to open them in a gesture of outreach and diversity? Do we hold to what we have, or do we risk relationship with **the whole world**? Jesus' parable of the talents was a story about faith and what individuals do with their faith. Do we unleash our beliefs for the world to witness, or keep them under wraps, hidden in protective security? Do we increase, or do we die?

Urban versus Rural

As men moved eastward they found a plain in Shinar and settled there (11:2)...**Then they said come let us build ourselves a city...** (11:4)

Hints occur early in the Bible regarding tension between nomadic/rural life and urban life, between the tent dwellers and the tower builders. This surfaced in Chapter 3 with Cain and the origin of urbanization. The thrust of the story is against urbanism and the arrogance of technology.

The Gate of God

Babylon originally called itself Bab-ili, which meant "gate of god." Using a pun, biblical writers imposed a less flattering label, *bālal,* which meant be confused.[36] In Revelation, Babylon is referred to as a "home for demons and a haunt for every evil spirit...for all the nations have drunk the wine of adulteries." (18:2-3) The writer of the last book of the Bible then links back to the original tower story: "But it was her sins that 'reached...into heaven' (18:5) In the concluding passages of Revelation, Babylon is contrasted with the holy city which comes, "down out of the heaven," whose open gates unite the nations (21:10-24-27).

Though not specifically stated, the reference in Revelation may have been to Jacob's dream at Bethel (Genesis 28:10-22). When Jacob awoke from his sleep he said, "Surely, the Lord is in this place, and I was not aware of it . . . . This is none other than the house of God; this is the gate of heaven."(16-17) Whether intended or not, the implication is that no tower is needed to reach God. God creates his own stairway to earth. God comes down. Had there been a tower, no vision would have occurred.

Another relevant and timely truth emerging from this story is that the gate to heaven, to God, is anywhere and everywhere. Analogous to the scattering of the peoples, God's spirit is omnipresent. This links with Pentecost when Peter, quoting the prophet Joel, says, "I will pour out my spirit on all people." God's spirit cannot be contained in one spot, insulated within the walls of any special place. This was a prominent message of Jesus, one of his attacks on the Jewish conception that God resided in the Holy of Holies within the inner sanctum of the Temple. Was this why he prophesied the destruction of the Temple? Was the fate of the Temple parallel to that of the Tower of Babylon? Following its destruction the Jews were scattered. What happens to religions when they become top heavy with pride, arrogance and possession of the knowledge of good and evil?

QUESTIONS FOR STUDY AND DISCUSSION

1. What are some "metaphors" for ways we attempt to build such towers?
2. What are some modern "Towers of Babel" which impede our spiritual growth?
3. What structures, complexes, organizations stand in the way to world peace? Would the U. S. military industrial complex be a "Tower of Babel?"
4. In our country's drive to keep ourselves safe have we isolated ourselves from much of the world in the way the early Babylonians felt they had to do?
5. Are current immigration policies and the conflicts surrounding them reminiscent of the ancient Babylonians who wanted to protect their culture and language, maintain a cultural purity?
6. What are the dangers of isolationism, of building walls? Make a list and discuss ways you and/or your group can bring them down.
7. What are our towers? What towers impede our spiritual vision?

Chapter Five

Abraham: Father of Monotheism

THE TEXT

The Call—Genesis 11:27-12:6

Terah became the father of Abram, Nahor and Haran . . . Abram and Nahor both married. The name of Abram's wife was Sarai . . . . Now Sarai was barren. Terah took his son Abram, his grandson Lot, son of Haran, and his daughter-in-law Sarai...and together they set out for Ur of the Chaldeans to go to Canaan. But when they came to Haran, they settled there. Terah lived 205 years and he died in Haran.

—Genesis 11:27, 30-32

The Lord said to Abram, leave your country, your people and your father's household and go to the land I will show you. I will make you a great nation, I will bless you, I will make your name great . . . . So Abram left, as the Lord had told him . . . . Abram was 75 years old when he set out from Haran. He took his wife Sarai . . . all the possessions that had accumulated in Haran, and they set out for the land of Canaan . . . .

—Genesis 12:1-5

54

The Covenant—Genesis 15:1-21 and 17:1-27

He also said to him, "I am the Lord, who brought you out of Ur of the Chaldeans to give you this land to take possession of it" . . . . On that day the Lord made a covenant with Abram and said, "To your descendants I give this land, from the river of Egypt to the great river, the Euphrates..." (15:7,18)

And when Abram was ninety-nine years old, the Lord appeared to him and said, "I am God Almighty, walk before me and be blameless. I will confirm my covenant between me and you and will greatly increase your numbers . . . . I will establish my covenant as an everlasting covenant between me and you and your descendants after you. The whole land of Canaan, where you are now an alien I will give as an everlasting possession to you and your descendants . . . and I will be their God.

—Genesis (17:1-2, 7-8

The Test—Genesis 22: 1-19

Sometime later God tested Abraham...God said, "Take your son, your only son, Isaac, whom you love, and go to the region of Moriah. Sacrifice him there as a burnt offering on one of the mountains I will tell you about." (22:1-2)

When they had reached the place God had told him about, Abraham built an altar there and arranged the wood on it. He bound his son Isaac and laid him on the altar on top of the wood. Then he reached out his hand and took the knife to slay his son.

But the angel of the Lord called out to him from heaven, "Abraham! Abraham! Do not lay a hand on the boy. (22:9-12)

The angel of the Lord called out to Abraham a second time and said, "I swear by myself, declares the Lord, that because you have done this and have not withheld your son, your only son, I will surely bless you and your descendants . . . ." (22:15-17)

The Peacemaker—Genesis 25: 7-10

Altogether, Abraham lived a hundred and seventy-five years. Then Abraham breathed his last and died at a good old age, an old man and full of years, and he was gathered to his people. His sons Isaac and Ishmael buried him . . . . (25:7-10)

THE CONTEXT

With Genesis 11:27 the Abraham saga and the story of Israel begin. The stories of Creation, the Fall, the Flood and the Tower of Babel serve as a prologue connecting the Creator of the earth with Hebrew history. Those stories serve functions discussed in previous chapters and prepare the way for the main feature, the birth and history of God's chosen people: Israel. When we turn the page from Genesis 11 to Genesis 12, we leave a prehistoric era and enter second millennium B.C.E. history and the stories of the patriarchs.

The story of the father of three major world religions opens abruptly with Genesis 11:26: **When Terah had lived 70 years he became the father of Abram, Nahor and Haran.** With this unpromising beginning, Abraham appears on the stage of world history. He comes from good stock, a productive family tree that extends back to Noah and ultimately the first human, Adam. Yet, Abraham is childless. We know little else about him. In contrast to other biblical heroes—Isaac, Ishmael, Moses, Joseph, David, and Jesus—scripture says nothing about Abraham's mother or his childhood. With other stories of the Bible, we glimpse something of their personality and character. With Abraham we read only **When Terah had lived 70 years he became the father of Abram...** When we meet Abraham he is in his seventies, an age when many modern men are fading. Abraham's future, and that of the people of Israel, opens with a call from God.

The Call

The critical point in this story is God's call to Abraham, a descendent of the Babel dispersion. Perhaps the reason so little is revealed about Abraham is God's previous disappointments. God is looking for someone without a history, someone new and fresh. Adam and Eve were failures in a special garden prepared for them. Ten generations later, God chose Noah, a righteous man, to rescue the corrupt, evil world. Although Noah succeeded in saving humanity and all forms of life by building an ark, he became drunk and turned to alcohol. After another ten generations, the humanity God created built a tower that reached to the heavens. This act was unacceptable to God, so he caused great confusion among his creatures and scattered them to the corners of the earth. From the beginning, God's "good" creations have yielded disappointing results, and he is ready for a change. He needs a new person, someone who will be faithful, obey his commands and value his blessings. God needs a man like Abraham:

> The Lord said to Abram, "Leave your country,
>
> your people and your father's household and
>
> go to the land I will show you. I will make you
>
> into a great nation and I will bless you. I will
>
> make your name great and you will be a blessing.
>
> I will bless those who bless you, and whoever
>
> curses you, I will curse; and all peoples on earth
>
> will be blessed through you.
>
> —Genesis 12:1-3

God's first words to Abraham are a summons to leave his home, his birthplace, and his father's home for a new country that would be shown to him. (Genesis 12:2-3). Abraham believes the Lord's promises—to possess land, to become a great nation, to be a blessing to peoples of the earth—and follows God's command to leave the homeland of his family. The patriarchs' migration begins as an act of faith. Throughout the journeys of the patriarchs, from Abraham to the conquest of Canaan, this three-fold promise surfaces. The promise to Abraham would become a twofold pledge to the patriarchs following him: 1) promise of the possession of the land of Canaan and, 2) the promise of unlimited and immeasurable posterity. This new type of history would bring blessings to the whole world. The pessimism pervading the Tower of Babel story suddenly brightens with optimism and a new day dawns. In contrast to the ego-maniacal tower-builders, God will make a name for Abraham, a man of faith, a name that will bless the whole world. Because of God's involvement in her history, Israel will become great.

The Covenant

Covenants as formal contracts between two parties were common in Abraham's time in the Near East. Often they were taken under oath and sealed. If the contracts were kept, parties were blessed. If they were broken, parties were cursed. God's covenant with Abraham in Genesis chapter 15, similar to those of his era, was broad and far-reaching. It included a son, land, a nation, a name, kings, descendants, and a blessing. The circumcision covenant of chapter 17 is viewed by most commentators as a revision of the earlier covenant in chapter 15. In this later passage, the promise is more focused on Abraham and less on the land. With Abraham, a covenant was more than an agreement or contract, it was a solemn promise made under oath. In the scripture, it is referenced with the rite of cutting animals. What God promises is not something to be obtained in the future. The land belongs to Abraham and his descendents at the time the promise is made. Ultimately, the promises focus on God's activity in and through a chosen people for the purpose of redemption.

Chapter 15 is in two segments. The first segment, verses 1-6, promise an heir to Abraham. The second, verses 8-21 add the promised land of Palestine. When Abraham asks, **Oh sovereign, how**

can I know that I will gain possession of it? Abraham's humanity surfaces. This man of faith has a question. Some argue that God should not be questioned. The opposite of faith, however, is not doubt but cynicism. The Lord recognizes that faith and doubt are part of the same process and in response to Abraham's question makes a covenant.

At first glance, the covenant seems imbalanced. God extends these multiple promises and nothing is required of Abraham. A closer read of the passage indicates God requires two things of Abraham. First, Abraham must leave his home, the place where he grew up, and go to a place not yet identified. This is an awesome demand. All Abraham knows from God is **the land I will show you.** (12:1). The second requirement of Abraham is equally challenging: "He must accept the legitimacy of the party offering the deal."[37] In other words, Abraham must not only believe *in* God, he must *believe* God. Abraham must take an existential leap of faith.

Whether the focus is on the covenant of chapter 15 or chapter 17, the theme of faithfulness is dominant and unchanged. The Lord's requirement of faithfulness from Abraham is central to the story (15:1-6; 12:1-9; 22:1-19) and is exemplified in the near sacrifice of Isaac. (26:3-5, 24) God's covenant with Abraham is bilateral. Abraham's future is not determined solely by the one giving the promises, but upon how the recipient of the promises responds. Abraham is not a passive but an active participant in God's plans and promises. Human freedom is involved. Abraham must make decisions. Each decision becomes a struggle as he evaluates the possibilities.

God's covenant with Abraham foreshadows His covenant with David. The covenant is founded upon God's election and saving actions. Faith is essential and Abraham and David are men of faith. Their parallel stories and themes bring the ancestral promise made by God to Abraham to fulfillment in the Christ.

The Test

The episode of Abraham and the binding of Isaac is story-telling at its best. The account is viewed by some as the centerpiece and culmination of the Abraham saga. The ideal short story format of character, event, and change is vividly developed. In this story the writer presents the two major characters with brief strokes and sufficient detail. The father and son relationship is revealed with touching clarity. With consummate artistry the tension mounts as the wood is gathered and arranged, the altar built, the child bound, the knife clasped. The action moves quickly then suddenly slows at verse 9. In verses 9-10 each movement becomes a snapshot, an individual moment arrested. This is particularly evident in verse 10 when the knife is grasped and raised and the angel stops the hand in mid-air. Following this dramatic event, the lives of both individuals are significantly changed. Abraham's faithfulness is strengthened. On the other hand, the passiveness of Isaac that emerges later in the patriarch narrative, may revert to this traumatic experience. Though a psychological analysis is impossible, there are arguably certain aspects of Isaac's personality as an adult that suggest post-traumatic stress elements.

Abraham's faithfulness to God is embodied in his willingness to sacrifice Isaac. In this story, the sacrifice of one's own child is portrayed as the supreme act of faith. Abraham is not commanded by God to kill his son but to offer him as a sacrifice. The nature of Abraham's faith is observed at the beginning of the passage when God calls his name and Abraham responds, **Here I am.** (Genesis 22:1) This same faith responded to God when he said to Abraham, **Leave your country . . .** (Genesis 12:1) and **Abraham left, as the Lord had told him . . . .** (12:4). In both instances there is no wavering. God calls, Abraham responds. There is no lapse of time, no procrastination. Abraham's faith immediately transforms into behavior. **Early the next morning, Abraham got up and saddled his donkey.** (22:3) His trust in God is complete. **God himself will provide.** (22:8) Throughout the passage, Abraham trusts. God had not disappointed him in the past; he will not disappoint him in finding a way to the future. And Abraham's object of faith, the plan God revealed to him, is always something in the future (Genesis 15:5-6).

Abraham is unaware he is being tested. "If Abraham had known in advance it was a test, it would have been no real test; for he (or anyone) would respond differently to a test from a more indirect method of discernment."[38] But another is being tested: God. Walter Brueggemann comments that the episode "is not a game with God; God genuinely does not know…The flow of the narrative accomplishes something in the awareness of God. He did not know. Now he knows."[39]

There is tension between Abraham and God. The storyteller shows the tension mounting. The test is real. Otherwise, Abraham's faith is a sham. Without his faith, Abraham is useless to God. But God says to him, **Now I know that you fear God because you have not withheld from me your son, your only son.** This part of the story allegedly took place on Mount Moriah, the home of the Rock, where Jesus worshipped and died. New Testament writers would later make the connection. Abraham's faith becomes the bridge to David and the messianic hope, God's only son.

The Peacemaker

Abraham's prominent position in Israel's history and the significance of his call, covenant, and faith qualify him as a key figure in the Judeo-Christian tradition, but he is also the father of Islam. Fourteen million Jews, two billion Christians, and a billion and a half Muslims claim history's first monotheist as their ancestor. "He is the linchpin of the Arab-Israeli conflict. He is the centerpiece of the battle between the West and Islamic extremists."[40]

In a panoramic sweep one can stand today on the Mount of Olives and view the Dome of the Rock, the Wailing Wall and the Church of the Holy Sepulcher. The city of Old Jerusalem, holy to three faiths, is where Solomon built the first Jewish temple, where Jesus walked and prayed and was crucified, and where Mohammed ascended into heaven. Within this modern geo-political context, Abraham looms more important and relevant in his death than in his life: **Then Abraham breathed his last and died . . . . His sons Isaac and Ishmael buried him . . . .** Ishmael, the prototype of Islam, and Isaac, the precursor of Israel stood side by side and buried their father. They may not have been shaking hands or embracing, but they came together and buried their father. The symbolic power of that gesture resonates in our troubled time. Abraham, the knight of faith, is also the potential knight of peace.

THE MESSAGE

The Call

Reflect for a moment upon this hypothetical situation: Your cell phone rings. The voice on the receiver says, "This is God. I want you and your family to pack all your belongings and leave the United States of America. You will be going to a far away land that I will show you later. You will become great, famous, and blessed. I will be good to all who are good to you and curse those who curse you. The whole world will be blessed through you." Click.

A wise sage once said, "If you don't take risks, you're not growing." Abraham's answer to God's call was the height of risk taking. What would you do if the Lord called? **Abram left, as the Lord told him..."** Could you pull up stakes, travel a great distance, start over? We might if the President of the United States, some high ranking official, or chief executive of a major corporation called.

"Where to?"

"Timbuktu, middle of the Sahara Desert, St. Helena Island . . . not sure . . . I'll tell you after you've packed and left town."

No problem, you think. I'll become great and famous, good things will happen to me and bad things to my enemies. Who could turn down that opportunity?

But it is not the President of the United States, some high ranking official, or chief executive. It is God calling. Pack your things, gather your family, and leave...NOW.

What would you do?

Abram left, as the Lord told him.

Abram is seventy-five years old when he takes an incredulous leap of faith and the Lord suddenly jump-starts his life. At his age and in that ancient time, we do not know if he had gout, arthritis, low back pain, prostrate problems. We do not know if he had all his teeth and used a staff to steady his gait. Scripture tells us he had lived and grown up in the village of Haran. We can imagine that when he stepped from his tent each morning his eyes touched the same familiar sights. He greeted people he met by name and he knew the names of their children. He followed a familiar daily routine. Then God called: "Pull up stakes, Abram, and leave. I have a plan for you."

Abram and Sarai could have done nothing. But they *chose* to respond to God's call and leave the comforts of their home. They made a conscious choice. Faith, the dominant theme of the Abraham saga, is about conscious choices in response to God's grace. Feeling and emotion are part of the human psychological makeup, but belief based solely upon feelings and moments of emotion is insubstantial and weak, given to whims of lapse. Faith operates from a position of strength when one *chooses* to believe there is a God. Credit rests not with the believer but with God, the Source of the option. Abram already believed in God. He had a foundation, so when God spoke, Abram *believed* him. "He doesn't *believe in* God; he *believes* God. He doesn't *ask for* proof; he *provides* the proof."[41] The decision to do as the Lord told him was automatic. Abraham's ultimate response was to devote himself to God. Abraham is considered to be the father of the Muslims. The word "Muslim" means "one who submits to God." In the tradition of Abraham, Christ, and St. Paul, to be a Christian is to answer God's call, take a voyage of faith.

Taking risks is not easy at any age and becomes more difficult as we grow older. "Not all of us are called to literally pack our belongings and move to a different location. Most of us would rather settle for what is known than to take a chance on the unfamiliar. However, discerning and following God's purposes may often mean personal inconvenience and putting other's needs before our own."[42] This comment from *The International Lesson* draws our attention to God's call and purpose for our lives in the 21st century.

In these uncertain economic times of industrial shutdowns, bank failures, shifting markets, and globalization, we hear frequently of employees being told they must move to a new location. Often these moves take place very quickly. Children are uprooted from the familiar world of friends and schools; adults are torn from supportive relationships and loved ones. Many of them could relate to Abraham.

With the first few verses of "the call," a story they know well unfolds. It is time to move on. Others have embarked on one career only to realize they made a mistake; they must make a change in the midstream of life. Successful men and women sometimes leave lucrative careers to enter the ministry. In these situations, the question for people of faith is ever present: What is God's will for me? What is God's purpose for me on this earth? This is the contemporary message of Abram's call.

God's call and purpose does not relate only to religious occupations. Abraham, Moses, and David were herders. Paul was a tanner. Jesus probably began as a carpenter. All of us have gifts, talents, and services we can render. "But each man has his own gift from God" (1 Corinthians 7:7). To ignore and squander these God-given attributes is a loss to the world that could be called a sacrilege or an act of selfishness. The decision of how to use the gift(s) requires spiritual listening, being tuned to God's word.

At this point, the reader might question the meaning of the statement. Each person must determine what is best for him or her. Some gain this insight from silence and listening. Moses, Abraham and Jesus went into the desert where it was quiet. For others, answers come through the discipline of daily prayer and devotion. Consultation with professionals and group discussions with others in a similar situation can be helpful. The message of Abram asserts God's call is there for each of us, but we must be receptive and disciplined to hear it.

The journey of faith for Abraham and Sarah receives attention in the New Testament. The writer of Hebrews describes how they, and others, " . . . were still living by faith when they died. They did not receive the things promised, they only saw them and welcomed them from a distance" (11:13). There are many blessings along the way, but fulfillment may not be accomplished in this lifetime. Keeping the faith in God's word is the important issue.

The Covenant

The Covenant with Abraham was initiated by God. It was God who spoke first, not Abraham. In the backwaters of the Near East God spoke and Abram heard. Several fundamental truths spring from this story and one among them is eternal companionship. The universe is not empty. We are not alone. As frail and weak as humanity seems at times, God, the Creator with His infinite strength is our "refuge and underneath are the everlasting arms" (Deuteronomy 33:27). When our focus fails, our courage falters, we must recall, with confidence, our covenant with Another. This note of covenant maintains a steady beat throughout the Old Testament. It begins with Abraham, continues with Moses (Exodus 34:27), and surfaces repeatedly with the prophets. In the New Testament the theme is picked up by Luke in Zachariah's Song ("to remember his holy covenant, the oath he swore to our father Abraham" (1:72) and Acts ("you are heirs of the prophets and of the covenant God made with your fathers"(3:25); by Paul (Romans 9:4 and 11:27; Galatians 3:15, 17; Ephesians 2:12, and extensively by the writer of Hebrews (8:6-10; 9:4; 10:16, 29; 12:24; 13: 20) The religious sages of both testaments knew the source of character, and it was not themselves, but a higher power.

Continuing the logic of the previous paragraph, not only are we not alone, but covenant generates the concept of partnership with God. His future intentions for the world depend upon the faithfulness of his creatures. God is not some abstract Ideal that must be please ' relationship with the world is incarnational, the ph··· are intermingled. A covenantal relationshi·   .ay, but inter-relational. What we do ··   world. Jesus expresses the New Testament,   ...it, concept when he says, "whatsoever you did for o.   ...e least of these brothers of mine, you did for me" (Matthew 25:40).

This segment of scripture about God's covenant with Abraham is about making and keeping promises. When we make promises, and the other party acknowledges expectation, we are in covenant. Covenants are about relationships. There are consequences for the making and keeping of promises. When people keep their promises with others, relationships thrive. When promises are broken, relationships die. The most common covenantal relationship we know is that of marriage. The steadily rising divorce rate points to the lack of seriousness that individuals place on their vows, their solemn oaths. Does this reflect on their relationship with God, their recognition of the covenantal obligations in that relationship? We cannot speak of Abraham's covenant with God without scrutinizing our own covenantal relationships. These include our spouse, children, neighbors, church, community, and the world at large. A covenant with God means a covenant with the world. This is an axiom of faith.

Covenantal theology as we know it began with Abraham. Its influence throughout western history has been profound. Its effects upon American history have been significant and little recognized. From the early democratic stirrings of the Enlightenment, to the Pilgrim's Mayflower Compact and its revolutionary Massachusetts descendents, the weight of Abraham's covenant with God has been felt. The early settlers of the Massachusetts Colony viewed their charter with the British Crown as one based upon covenantal principles binding upon both parties. When the Crown broke its pledge, the people of Massachusetts launched their own revolution and closed every court in the colony, two years before Lexington and Concord.[43] An argument can be made that covenantal theology and the concept of covenantal contract which originated with Abraham was a contributing factor in the American Revolution. Our Founding Fathers even described America as a "New Promised Land" and spoke of "a covenant with God."

The Test

The audience at a circus does not gather to watch acrobats swing on a trapeze, but to see the critical moment when the performer releases one trapeze bar to catch the next swinging toward her. In *Fear and Trembling,* a book Danish theologian Søren Kierkegaard called one of the most perfect he had written, Abraham is portrayed as the "knight of faith" who releases the trapeze.[44] The book is developed around Abraham's sacrifice of Isaac. The situation with Isaac is not his only test. The story begins with a test. Abraham releases from a comfortable position without knowing another will be there to take its place. In faith, and with a promise from God, Abraham lets go. But, "The Test" biblical authorities consider to be the most significant for Abraham is the Isaac event on Mount Moriah.

The story of Abraham's near sacrifice of Isaac was not placed in the Old Testament because human sacrifice, an actual practice among some Canaanite tribes,[45] was prohibited for the religion of the Israelites. The story is in the scriptures to reflect the extent Abraham demonstrated his faith. It is a story of religion at the edge, at its farthest reach, its highest passion. It is a portrayal of faith at its extreme point of commitment. It is the precursor of another sacrifice by another Father. It is a foreshadowing of the Crucifixion of Christ.

The story is told of a train switchman who serviced the tracks near his home. From the vantage point of one brake switch, he could see the track in the distance where it crossed a river trestle. His role was to switch the tracks when another train was coming, allowing one train to side track. One day, as a passenger train rapidly approached, the switchman observed with dismay his small son playing on the trestle tracks. The side track on the trestle was in repair. If he swung the switch, the train, filled with travelers, would plunge into the river canyon. The train was bearing down, his son trapped in its path. The switchman made his swift decision. The passengers were saved.

In this story a son *was* sacrificed. In the bible story the word of God, at the last second, aborted a sacrifice. A story that could have ended in tragedy, concluded with harmony and oneness between a man and his God. We can only ponder the outcome if the results had been different. One lesson for us from this story is posed as a question: Would we be willing to pay the ultimate price when our conscience tells us it is the right thing to do? The switchman did. He sacrificed his son for the lives of others. Our faith tells us that if God does permit suffering, as he did on Calvary, He identifies with our sacrifice and suffering and we are redeemed.

Faith is the core message of the Abraham epic. "Yet Abraham believed and did not doubt, he believed the preposterous."[46] Abraham obeyed because he had faith. This is clearly indicated in verse 8: **"God himself will provide the lamb for the burnt offering, my son," and the two of them went on together.** God will not disappoint Abraham. Abraham left Haran, not because he was commanded by God, but because he trusted God. With Isaac on Mount Moriah, Abraham trusts God, he does not follow a command. Abraham trusts God unto, and through, death. The writer of *Hebrews* injects the theme of Resurrection: "By faith, Abraham when God tested him, offered Isaac as a sacrifice. He who had received the promises was about to sacrifice his one and only son, even though he had said to him, 'It is through Isaac that your suffering will be reckoned. Abraham reasoned that God could raise the dead, and figuratively speaking, he did receive Isaac back from death" (11:17-19).

In the New Testament Christ mirrors Abraham. Jesus is tested and he remains faithful. Jesus believes God would be faithful in his promises. The Garden of Gethsemane was the crucial test and Jesus took the cup. On the third day God delivered on his promise. The Redeemer, because He was tested, is able to help others in their time of testing. In 1 Corinthians 10:13 Paul says, "No temptation has seized you except what is common to man. And God is faithful, he will not let you be tempted beyond what you can bear. But when you are tempted, he will also provide a way out so that you can stand up under it." (cf. Hebrews 2:18; 4: 15) An old spiritual song comes to mind, "Nobody knows the troubles I've seen, nobody knows but Jesus." From another Old Testament perspective, "Even though I walk through the valley of the shadow of death, I will fear no evil, for you are with me" (Psalm 23:4).

The Peacemaker

Death has several positive aspects. It is a catalyst of creativity and accomplishment. Dying reduces the tension between old age and youth and allows space for the succeeding generations. Death also heals. Funerals have a way of bringing people together. People who have been estranged and alienated must face each other again. This is especially true of siblings when the deceased is their last parent.

In his death, Abraham fosters peace. Two of his sons had been rivals before they were even born, alienated almost seventy-five years since childhood. "Abraham achieves in death what he could never achieve in life: a moment of reconciliation between his two sons, a peaceful, communal, side-by-side flicker of possibility in which they are not rivals, scions, warriors, adversaries, children, Jews, Christians, Muslims."[47] We do not know what words were spoken, whether they shook hands, hugged, or just stood side by side. Scripture does say that Isaac and Ishmael came together when their father died and that they cooperated in his burial.

At its beginning, the story of Abraham is the story of the beginning of Israel. At its conclusion, ironically, and symbolically relevant for our time, Israel is joined by others, primarily Ishmael. The powerful symbolism of this event in ancient history resonates into the 21st century. Today, the ancestors of Abraham, the father of three faiths, are killing each other and burying their own. If Abraham were alive, he would certainly disapprove.

In March of 2000, Pope John Paul II made a pilgrimage to the Holy Land and visited the Wailing, or Western Wall. Consistent with the custom of pilgrims who visit the sacred place, he touched one of the massive stones. Then, with a feeble and trembling hand he placed a small piece of paper folder several times over in one of the crevices. On the paper was a prayer which was later retrieved and placed in the Yad Vashem Holocaust museum in Jerusalem. More than any document of our era, Pope John Paul II's holy petition is a ringing manifesto for peace:

> God of our fathers, you chose Abraham and his descendants
>
> to bring your name to the nations. We are deeply saddened
>
> by the behavior of those who in the course of history have
>
> caused these children of yours to suffer. And asking your
>
> forgiveness, we wish to commit ourselves to genuine
>
> brotherhood with the people of the covenant.[48]

We hope against hope for the fulfillment of this prayer, that Jew, Muslim, and Christian would come together. Though differences have emerged over the years, the three religions share a common heritage. Much within their religious concepts either coincide are relate tangentially. One hopeful outcome of Bruce Feiler's best-seller, *Abraham, A Journey to the Heart of Three Faiths,* has been the creation of "the Abraham Initiative," a growing movement in which

Jews, Muslims, and Christians, in communities within this country and abroad, are gathering and engaging in dialogue about their commonalities and differences.

The world needs Abraham. The world needs his trust, his resolve, his vision, his covenant. The scripture harbors the hopeful prophesy that the sons of Abraham, Jew and Muslim, will sit down at a table prepared for them (Psalm 23: 5) and rediscover their inheritance and the universal dimension of his covenant, which is God's blessings to all people, for all humanity.

QUESTIONS FOR FURTHER STUDY AND DISCUSSION

1. How would you respond if God called you today to travel to some unknown destination?
2. What is God's purpose for you? How can you discern God's will for your life?
3. Have you experienced a call from God? If so, how did you respond?
4. In the story of Abraham, the concept of covenant is placed in theological terms. What are the covenants that affect our daily lives? Are they taken as seriously as our covenant with God?
5. In the story about the train switchman, what would you have done?
6. Name some shared beliefs among Jews, Muslims and Christians?
7. If all three faiths are represented in your community, try to assemble a group and discuss common beliefs, hopes and aspirations? (You can each claim Abraham as the father of your faith.)

Chapter Six

Moses: Leader and Law-Giver

THE TEXT

The Call (Burning Bush)—Exodus 3:1-4:17

>Now Moses was tending the flock of Jethro, his father-in-law . . . and he led the flock to the far side of the desert and came to Horeb, the mountain of God. There the angel of the Lord appeared to him in flames of fire from within a bush . . . . When the Lord saw that he had gone over to look, God called to him from within the bush, "Moses! Moses!
>
>And Moses said, "Here I am."
>
>"Do not come any closer," God said. "Take off your sandals, for the place where you are standing is holy ground . . . . The Lord said, "I have indeed seen the misery of my people, I have heard them crying out . . . . So now go, I am sending you to Pharaoh to bring my people the Israelites out of Egypt."
>
>So Moses said to God, "Suppose I go to the Israelites and say to them, 'The God of your fathers has sent me to you, and they ask me, 'What is his name?' Then what shall I tell them?"
>
>God said to Moses, "*I am who I am.* This is what you are to say to the Israelites: *I am* has sent me to you."
>
>—Genesis 3:1-2, 4-5, 7, 10, 13-14

The Passover and Exodus—12:12-14:31

On that same night I will pass through Egypt and strike down every first-born . . . and will bring judgment on all of the gods of Egypt . . . . This is the day you are to commemorate; for the generations to come you shall celebrate it as a festival . . . . "

—Genesis 12:12, 14

Then Moses stretched out his hand over the sea and all that night the Lord drove the sea back with a strong east wind and turned it into dry land. The waters were divided and the Israelites went through the sea on dry ground with a wall of water on their right and on their left.

—Genesis 14:21-22

The Law-Giver—Exodus 20:1-31:18

And the Lord spoke all these words:

"You shall have no other gods before me.

You shall not make for yourselves an idol...

You shall not misuse the name of the Lord...

Remember the Sabbath day by keeping it holy...

Honor your father and your mother...

You shall not murder.

You shall not commit adultery.

You shall not steal.

You shall not bear false testimony against your neighbor.

You shall not covet . . . . "

—Exodus 20: 1, 3-4, 7-8, 12-17

The Context

Moses is the preeminent personality of the Old Testament, surpassing King David in the influence and esteem of the Jewish people. Some say David was more important than Moses, but without Moses there would be no Ark, no Tabernacle, and no Temple. He is the centerpiece of a significant section of the Old Testament and the architect of the Mosaic Law. Moses is the pivotal figure in the Old Testament and history of Israel and a precursor of the New Testament, or New Covenant, and Jesus Christ.

In the New Testament, numerous references are made to Moses and the Mosaic Law. Of all the giants of the Old Testament, Moses was considered the most influential on Christianity. Moses and his accomplishments laid the foundation for the nation of Israel and ultimately, the messianic concept.

According to the Bible, primarily the Pentateuch, the Israelites were led from the land of Egypt by Moses and established themselves in the Land of Canaan. This is the beginning of the history of Israel as a nation, told in bold drama and extravagant detail.

Was there a man named Moses who led his people out of Egypt? Was there a forty year journey through the wilderness of Sinai? Did the ten plagues of Egypt happen? Did the bush burn, the waters part, and the bread fall from heaven? These are stunning questions to those of us raised on the traditional Bible stories. These questions are being raised today, not only by Christians, but also by Jewish scholars. Research has provided challenging scholarship and new information that tests our faith and helps us rethink and reinterpret scripture.

Historians speculate about whether or not Moses was an actual person. We are not historians. Our objective is not to prove or disprove history. Our objective is to re-evaluate the testimonies of our faith as they are presented in the stories of the Old Testament. Whether Moses was man or myth parallels whether Adam was man or myth. The emphasis falls not on the man but the truths of the stories surrounding him. Whether Moses actually existed and led the Israelites from Egypt to the Promised Land is not as important to us as the words which testify to the faith of the man and the People. Those words, those stories, are metaphors, vehicles of faith which inform and inspire faith.

The birth and early childhood of Moses are swept aside by the awesome role he assumed in leading the People of Israel out of Egyptian bondage. The exodus from Egypt was interpreted by Israel's faith as representing the height of God's grace, power and faithfulness. This viewpoint dominated Jewish theology into the Christian era where it became of great importance to the early church. The theme surfaces throughout the New Testament, but a few examples are noteworthy. In the transfiguration story, Luke uses the word *exodus* when Moses and Elijah are discussing Christ's death (9:30-31) Regardless of the exact date of Christ's death, it occurred during the Passover and within the context of that great feast. Paul refers to Christ as the Passover Lamb (1 Corinthian 5:7). The writer of the Gospel of John hints at the same identification by stressing that no bones of Christ were broken on the cross. (John 19:33, 36). In Exodus 12:46 no bone must be broken of the Passover lamb. Passover was the beginning of the feast of unleavened bread. Paul states in 1 Corinthians 5:6-8 that Christians are to partake of "the bread of sincerity and truth."

The association of the exodus with redemption was a carryover from the Jewish faith and not a later invention of the Church. For Paul, Christ's death is a New Covenant sacrifice (1 Corinthians 11:25) sealed by God's blood as it sealed the Old Covenant in the Exodus story (Exodus 24:6). The Old Covenant is not destroyed, but fulfilled in Christ (Matthew 5:17). In the final pages of the New Testament the redeemed sing the song of Moses and the Lamb when they rise. To understand the New Testament, one must first understand the Exodus and its epic stories.

The Call: The Burning Bush

The story of Moses, like that of Jesus, moves quickly from birth to manhood. The narrative includes the fascinating story of the Pharaoh's daughter who found him in a basket in the bulrushes where his mother had hidden him for safety. **She named him Moses, saying, "I drew**

him out of the water." (2:10) He was raised as the Princesses' child with his birth mother as his nurse. He was reared in the Pharaoh's household where he was considered a prince. In the next few verses Moses is an adult, a murderer, an outcast, a lover and a husband. One perceives the writer moving toward a moment of great significance on which the entire saga will turn.

While tending the flock of Jethro, his father-in-law, Moses circled the desert **and came to Horeb, the mountain of God. There the angel of the Lord appeared to him in flames of fire from within a bush. (3:1b-2a)** Moses is struck by the phenomenon, a bush that is burning yet untouched by the flames. He ventures closer for a better look and the Lord speaks to him from the bush, **Moses, Moses.** Similar to Abraham (Genesis 22:11) and later the prophet Samuel (1 Samuel 3:10) Moses responds **Here I am.** The Lord instructs Moses to come no closer and to remove his sandals for he is standing on holy ground.

After establishing his legitimacy as the **God of Abraham, the God of Isaac, and the God of Jacob,** the Lord declares his purpose to Moses who is ready and willing to follow, his subservience reflected in the removal of his sandals. The Lord speaks to Moses from the bush in a conversational voice and tells Moses he has observed the slavery of the Hebrew people in Egypt and heard their cries. He has determined they should be rescued and delivered to a **land flowing with milk and honey.** The inhabitants of the land are identified—Canaanites, Hittites, Amorites, Jebusites, etc. The Lord says Moses is the man who should go and lead them. This is an order not a request, and Moses questions his own ability, **who am I that I should go . . . ? And God said, "I will be with you."**

The crux of the episode is in the passage that follows:

> **Suppose I go to the Israelites and say to them,**
>
> **"The God of your fathers has sent me to you,"**
>
> **and they ask me, "What is his name?" Then what**
>
> **shall I tell them?**
>
> **God said to Moses, "I am who I am. This is what**
>
> **you are to say to the Israelites: 'I am' sent me to**
>
> **you."**
>
> —Exodus 3:13-14

The Lord further states that this is His name for perpetuity. (3:15b) The name which means, "I AM," is the Hebrew word for God or Yahweh. It means literally, "I am that I am." It can also mean, "I cause to be what I cause to be." The origin of the name Yahweh is explained in greater detail in the "Exegesis" segment (See Appendix B), but the importance of this episode cannot be over-emphasized. This God is the Creator. He causes things to happen. The God of Genesis understands and is aware of what is happening in Egypt.

God then unveils his plan. First, Moses is to give authority to his mission by evoking God's name. Second he is to **assemble the elders of Israel,** an indication of an existing political framework in bondage. Third, Moses and the elders are to go to the pharaoh and tell him that **the Lord God of the Hebrews has met with us.** Fourth, Moses and the elders are to take **a three-day journey into the desert to offer sacrifices to the Lord our God** (3:18b). The Lord knows the pharaoh will not release the Hebrews and says, **I will stretch out my hand and strike the Egyptians with all the wonders that I will perform among them** (3:19) and the plagues to follow are foretold. With the Lord's directive firmly in mind, Moses returns to Jethro who frees him to return to his people in Egypt. The writer(s) have laid the groundwork for the Passover and eventual exodus, stamped with God's authoritative and powerful name: YHWH.

The Passover and the Exodus

The Passover and the Exodus represent an association of a ceremonial legend with a legendary event. They were interdependent in their historical occurrence and have become inseparable over time. For Jews, salvation was the Exodus and the event that marked their deliverance from slavery. The Exodus is now celebrated as the Feast of Unleavened Bread. For Christians, salvation is the resurrection of Christ and deliverance from death and is celebrated as Holy Communion or The Lord's Supper. Again, the roots of Christianity extend deep into Hebrew history. The stories of the Old Testament continue to resurrect in the New Testament.

Passover is associated with the last of the ten plagues God inflicted upon Egypt when the first-born of each household died and the death angel 'passed over' the Hebrew households marked by the blood of the Lamb. Through Moses, God instructed the Israelites that on the tenth day of their first month **each man is to take a lamb for his family, one for each household** (12:3) and care for the animal until **the fourteenth day of the month, when all the people of the community of Israel must slaughter them at twilight.** (12:6) The Israelites were further instructed on that evening to mark the doorposts of their homes with the blood of the slaughtered lambs. The blood on the door would be a sign to the spirit of the Lord to pass over those homes and spare their first-born. This was the final stroke for Pharaoh, and he finally gave the word to release the Hebrews and let them go. Tradition reports they departed in great haste, before their bread could rise, which is why no leavened bread can be eaten during the celebration of Passover, also called the Feast of Unleavened Bread.

After plundering the Egyptians **for articles of silver and gold and for clothing,** (12:35) the Israelites, approximately six hundred thousand men plus women and children, took their belongings and herds and left Egypt. The day of their departure was commemorated by the consecration of first born because the Lord said to Moses, **the first offspring of every womb among the Israelites belongs to me, whether man or animal.** The Lord further instructed them to commemorate their deliverance from slavery by eating unleavened bread for seven days when they arrived in Canaan and to hold a festival on the seventh day. In addition to that sacred ordinance, the Israelites were to give over to the Lord the firstborn of every womb as a sacrifice because the first-born of every Egyptian was killed.

The route of the Exodus was toward the Red Sea. The departing Hebrews were led by the Lord during the day by **a pillar of cloud . . . and by night in a pillar of fire.** (13:21) When Pharaoh realized his error in allowing six hundred thousand of his work-force to leave, he summoned his army and pursued the Israelites whose back was to the sea. Following the Lord's commands, Moses **stretched out his hand over the sea, and all that night the Lord drove the sea back with a strong east wind and turned it into dry land and the Israelites went through the sea on dry ground, with a wall of water on their right and on their left.** (14:21-22) Following again the Lord's command, Moses stretched out his hand over the sea and **at day break the sea went back to its place.** (14:27) The Pharaoh's army was destroyed. The Israelites were saved.

All nations can point to a crucial point in their history when they became a self-conscious community. With England, it may have been the Battle of Hastings. Mexicans point to September 16, 1810, when a priest, Miguel Gregorio Antonio Hidalgo, rang his parish church's bells and distributed his *Grito de Dolores* among them. For the United States of America the turning point may have been in 1777 at the Battle of Saratoga. The decisive event for Israel's history was the Exodus from Egypt. Centuries passed before the Hebrews became a nation, but at that point its people became a community of faith. Bernard Anderson draws the following parallel: "Just as the Christian remembers and relives the sacrifice of Jesus Christ in the celebration of the Lord's Supper, so the Jew recalls and makes contemporary the Exodus as he celebrates the Passover."[49]

Israel's beginning is not traced back to Abraham and his wilderness wonderings before coming to Canaan, but to Moses and the Exodus. In the eighth century B.C.E. the prophet Amos tells his listeners: "Hear the word the Lord has spoken against you, O people of Israel—against the whole family I brought you up out of Egypt. You only have I chosen of all the families of the earth." (3:1-2)

To date, no extra-biblical evidence of the Exodus has been discovered, but we do have the impressive witness of the Bible. Something happened and it created a community of people. "It is therefore natural that the exodus from Egypt, interpreted by Israel's faith as being the supreme example of God's grace, faithfulness and power, dominated all the thought of later Israel"[50] Today, over three millennia later, the Exodus is the core confession of faith of the Jewish religion. It is an event evoked repeatedly, like the theme of a great symphony, throughout the Old and into the New Testament where it lives again in the resurrected Christ.

The Law-Giver

Much happened to Moses and his band of followers before they reached Mount Sinai and none of it is incidental. That background is important in understanding the Hebrews' roller-coaster of faith that led to the appearance of the Ten Commandments and numerous additional laws, regulations, and rituals. The narrative description is of a people struggling to survive, "to find water and food, to discover the way, to hold an oasis, to preserve unity and order within the ranks, to escape annihilation by foes."[51] Their deliverance from the Egyptians at the Red Sea, or Sea of Reeds, was not the miracle that saved them. They were not, at that point, a transformed people. Like others before them—Abraham, Isaac, Jacob, Joseph—their faith continued to be tested. They were not yet the people God desired, the people he had carried **on eagle's wings** (Exodus 19:4).

The fifteenth day of their journey, **the whole Israelite community set out from Elim and came to the desert of Sin** (16:1). They became hungry and began to grumble. **That evening quail came and covered the camp, and in the morning there was a layer of dew around the camp** (16:13). The dew evaporated leaving thin flakes of bread the Hebrews called manna and ate for forty years until they reached Canaan. The manna had a special quality. It would last for only a day and hoarding it was a sin. Enough was provided on the sixth day for the Sabbath. Moses and Aaron told the Israelites this was done, so they **will know that it was the Lord who brought you out of Egypt** (16:6).

Leaving the Desert of Sin, the **whole Israelite community** traveled from place to place until they made camp at Rephidim where the people grumbled again because there was no water. Moses struck a rock at Horeb (Sinai) and water came forth. Shortly after this incident, at Rephidim the Israelites were attacked by the Amalekites. Moses stood on a hill and in a gesture similar to one used at the Red Sea, he raised his hand. **As long as Moses held up his hands, the Israelites were winning, but whenever he lowered his hands, the Amalekites were winning. When Moses' hands grew tired, they took a stone and put it under him and he sat on it."** A touch of comedy pervades this story, but the central element, as it was at the parting of the Red Sea, is Moses' faith. Amidst the waxing and waning of the people's belief, Moses' faith in the Lord is steadfast.

The next event, often overlooked, sets up the event of the Ten Commandments and subsequent body of laws governing the Israelites. Jethro, a priest of Midian and father-in-law of Moses pays a visit. He marvels at the mighty works of God on behalf of the people but is less impressed when he observed Moses serving as judge of the entire community, resolving every dispute. Jethro told Moses, **what you are doing is not good . . . The work is too heavy for you; you cannot handle it alone** (18:18). Then these words from the Midian priest:

> **You must be the people's representative before**
>
> **God and bring their disputes to him. Teach them**
>
> **the decrees and laws and show them the way to live**
>
> **and the duties they are to perform. But select capable**
>
> **men…and appoint them as judges for the people at**
>
> **all times.**
>
> —Genesis 18:19-22

And the scripture reports **Moses listened to his father-in-law and did everything he said.** (18:24)

In the third month since the exodus from Egypt, **and on that very day,** the Israelites departed Rephidim and entered the Desert of Sinai and pitched their tents at the foot of the mountain of God. The writer(s) has carefully orchestrated events and set the stage for the main event: The Ten Commandments and the beginning of the law and order.

Moses goes up and God calls to him from the mountain:

> **Now if you obey me fully and keep my covenant, then**
>
> **out of all nations you will be my treasured possession.**
>
> **Although the whole earth is mine, you will be for me a**
>
> **kingdom of priests and a holy nation. These are the**
>
> **words you are to speak to the Israelites.**
>
> —Genesis 19:5-6

Moses returns to the people and the people agree. At the Lord's command, Moses' then consecrates the people. In a gesture resembling a form of baptism or purification rite by water, the people wash their clothes. **Prepare yourselves for the third day. Abstain from sexual relations. On the morning of the third day there was thunder and lightning, with a thick cloud over the mountain, and a very loud trumpet blast. Everyone in the camp trembled.** (19:16)

The following scene is one of awesome power. With trumpet fanfare the Lord descends in fire onto Mount Sinai and smoke **billowed up from it like smoke from a furnace, the whole mountain trembled violently and the sound of the trumpet grew louder.** (19:18-19). No dramatist could have choreographed more effectively the entry onto the world stage of the Ten Commandments. (Exodus 20:1-17; Deuteronomy 5:1-21;)

The Ten Commandments

Moses and the Ten Commandments are synonymous. We cannot think of one without the other. But often lost and overshadowed are the multitude of laws, decrees, rulings, rituals, and regulation that accompanied the famous law code and its recipient. In fact, the book of Exodus contains more law than legend to the point the law itself attains a legendary status.[52]

Following the presentation of the Ten Commandments in Chapter 20, the Lord says to Moses, **These are the laws you are to set before them** (21:1), a catalogue which blankets daily life and worship: Hebrew servants (21:2-11); personal injuries (21:12-36); protection of property (22:1-15); social responsibility (22:16-31); laws of justice and mercy (23:1-9); Sabbath laws (23:10-13); the three annual festivals—Feast of Unleavened Bread, Feast of Harvest, and Feast of Ingathering—(23:14-19); offerings for the Tabernacle (25:1-9); the Ark, its construction, dimensions, covering, etc.(25:10-22); the construction and purpose of the Tabernacle Table for **the bread of the Presence** (25:23-30); the lampstand (25:31-40); construction and layout of the Tabernacle (26:1-37); The altar of burnt offering (27:1-8); the courtyard for the Tabernacle (27:9-19); oil for the lampstand (27:20-21); the priestly garments (28:1-5); the Ephod (28:8-14); the breastpiece (28:15-30); other priestly garments (28:31-43); consecration of the priests (29:1-46); the altar of incense (30:1-10); atonement money (30:11-16); basin for washing (30:17-21); anointing oil (30:22-33); incense (30:34-38); and a final admonition to **observe my Sabbath. This will be a sign between me and you for the generations to come, so you may know that I am the Lord, who makes you holy.** (31:12-13) Failure to keep the Sabbath was severe: death. **When the Lord finished speaking to Moses on Mount Sinai, he gave him the two tablets of the testimony, the tablets of stone inscribed by the finger of God.** (31:18)

THE MESSAGE

The Call

The Old Testament is filled with examples of God's call to all types of leaders. "Abraham . . . Moses, Moses . . . Samuel, Samuel . . . !" (Genesis 22:1; Exodus 3:4; Samuel 3:10) And they respond, "Here I am." From Abram in Genesis(12:1-5) to Isaiah (6:1-8) the list includes prophets, priests, kings, and judges. "The call" came in different ways, but, in each case, God had a mission and each mission required someone of faith. Each of these individuals were known by God and "called" by name. This theme is so pervasive in the scriptures the Bible could be entitled, *The Book of The Called.*

Moses' "Call" by God from the burning bush to confront Pharaoh and demand release of his people is a key event in the Exodus narrative. At first Moses was overwhelmed and resisted. He expressed his inability and his unworthiness. Other great religious leaders have voiced similar feelings when confronted with God's call. The Bible and Judeo-Christian history contain many examples. It is difficult for any person to stand in the presence of God, the Creator of the cosmos, and feel worthy. But, when God calls God empowers, a testament of faith dramatically demonstrated in the story of Moses.

God's call to the heroes of old can be overwhelming for those living in the 21st century, a time of population explosion, over-crowding, urban sprawl, and identity diffusion. We hardly expect the Creator of billions to know us by name. With the click of a computer key or retrieval of trash from a garbage bin, our identity is stolen, and our savings and credit are gone. With cell phones, i-pods, internet "face-books," call-waiting, and automatic dial, anyone can call us any time. How would a call from God get through? With that confusion of networks and noise, plus the hoards of humans covering the planet, a call "from God" seems improbable, against the odds.

We use the word "call" daily. The phrase is common parlance: What is your calling in life? Perhaps we can remember a particular moment we experienced a "call" to move in a certain direction, a vocation, a mate, church, or school. Perhaps there were other, follow-up, calls linking back to that original call.

For the Old Testament heroes, "the call" was not once and for all. God's covenant with Abraham, Moses, David, and the people of Israel was not a "done deal." Heeding God's call required a constant recommitment of faith, a continuous dialogue with the Lord. God's call was not one way. The spiritual masters of scripture persistently sought Him. "I call to you, O Lord, every day" (Psalms 88:9); "Then will I . . . fulfill my vows day after day" (Psalm 61:8); "For day after day they seek me out . . . . " (Isaiah 58:2) Believing in, and being receptive to, God's call is a daily exercise. On a daily basis, we must respond, a theme continued in the New Testament. "If anyone would come after me, he must deny himself and take up his cross daily and follow me" (Luke 9:23). "I die daily," Paul said. (1 Corinthians 15:31). In another letter he wrote, "Pray without ceasing" (1 Thessalonians 5:17, *King James Version*) God's call to people of faith is continuous and people must be continuously receptive.

An improbability of success was another interesting aspect of biblical heroes called by God. They were the least likely candidates to achieve something great. They became priests, kings, prophets, and judges but before God's call they were individuals of insignificant status. Most were rural-types without wealth, prestige, or power. **Who am I that I should go to Pharaoh . . . .** (Exodus 3:11) In this chapter, God calls Moses, a man with a brief and unimpressive resume. He is married, has killed a man, and is employed as a shepherd. Then Moses' life is changed. He hears a voice from a burning bush, a bush that is not consumed, and from this one event comes a life mission.

Throughout scripture God calls ordinary people to life missions. He knows their name and calls them by name. This thread is picked up in the New Testament where God continues calling people through His Son, Jesus Christ, to the mission of announcing the coming of His Kingdom and the establishment of His Church (the body of Christ) on earth. This is seen particularly in Jesus's calling of the twelve disciples and his final commission to them. They were not called from the synagogue where he often went and taught, but from daily life. The God of the Old Testament who called from a burning bush, a cloud, mountain tops, comes down to earth in the person of Jesus of Nazareth and calls personally. This shepherd knows each of his flock by name.

God called the heroes of antiquity, Jesus called disciples, and God still calls in a variety of ways and for a wide-range of ministries. As Paul notes in 1 Corinthians (12:1-11) and Ephesians (4:11-13), some are called by God to be apostles, some teachers, some prophets, administrators, healers. God's call that came from a burning bush long ago and burst forth anew in Christ continues today through the Holy Spirit.

As with Moses, an assurance accompanies the call: **I will be with you.** (3:12) No theme is more prominent: **I will be with you.** "Though

I walk through the valley of the shadow of death . . . you are with me." (Psalms 23:4) "And surely I am with you always, to the very end of the age." (Matthew 28:20) "The one who has sent me is with me, he has not left me alone."(John 8:29) " . . . nor anything else in all creation, will be able to separate us from the love of God that is in Christ Jesus our Lord." (Romans 8:39)

Another aspect of God's call in the story of Moses and the burning bush relates to God's approachability. In the story of the burning bush, the presence of God on earth speaks volumes. In the Garden of Eden and Tower of Babel stories, God demonstrated his willingness to come near and mingle with his earthlings, a foreshadowing of the Incarnation of Christ.

But humankind must keep a distance. Curiosity draws Moses closer to the bush for scrutiny and the Lord says, "Do not come any closer." (Exodus 3:5) In the Gospel of John, Jesus says to Thomas, "Do not hold onto me for I have not yet returned to the Father." (20:17) Later, Thomas is invited to touch him. (21:27) Following the burning bush experience, Moses will approach God and "come near" to intercede for others. (Ex. 32:30) Throughout the scriptures, a dynamic tension of God's nearness and distance is maintained, at times paradoxically—he is closest when he seems most distant. The crucifixion is a prime example of this paradox of faith.

God calls Moses, and Moses calls back. He asks God his name and God, the first existentialist, responds **I am who I am.** God's name is too sacred to be pronounced. The sacredness of his name corresponds to the sacredness of his Presence. Moses must remove his sandals. He is on holy ground because **I AM** was present. Holy ground and holy name are inseparable. If the name were not holy, the place would not be holy. A sacred place is created by a sacred name. We turn our attention at this point to the name.

The phrase, **I am who I am,** in Hebrew can also be interpreted to mean "I cause to be what I cause to be." The God who speaks from a burning bush is also the same God who breathed across the formless and empty dark and **created the heavens and the earth.** (Genesis 1:1) This is a God of power and energy, who makes things happen. He is what he is by what he does and accomplishes a hint of what God expects of us. "If the name of the God I worship is I Am, it seems to follow that only through what I am can I worship him aright."[53] We are created in His image. We are what we are. But we also cause to be what we cause to be. Our creative response to God's call identifies us as people of faith. We must make decisions. Faith may be based to some degree on experience and feeling, but the act of faith, of believing is a conscious choice. The French existentialist Jean Paul Sartre said, "We become our choices." We are called; we must *choose* to follow.

When Jesus uttered his famous "I am" sayings he was linking to Yahweh of the burning bush, to **I am that I am.** He was describing himself and his mission; he was identifying himself with God: "I am the bread of life that came down from heaven" (John 6:41), reminding us of the manna that God provided the people in their 40 years of wandering in the wilderness. In addition Jesus refers to himself as "the light of the world" (John 8:12), "I am the gate for the sheep" (John 10:7), "I am the good shepherd" (John 10:11), "I am the resurrection and the life" (John 11:25) and "I am the way, the truth and the life" (John 14:6). I am the I am. His name was holy; wherever he went became holy ground, attested to today by an area called "the Holy Land" and the many churches there built over, or near, the events of his ministry. In the scene where Jesus walks on water (Matthew 14:22-23; Mark 6:45-51; John 6:15-21) the translated words he speaks to the distressed disciples are. "Take Courage! It is I. Don't be afraid." But in the Greek the words are *ego eimi*, **I am I am.**

In addition to the Holy Land and its sacred places. what is holy ground in our 21st century world? Today, before entering a Muslim mosque, shoes must be removed. In some churches a woman's head must be covered and men must remove their hats. These are all signs of reverence, a symbolic gesture signifying that the place they are about to enter is holy. When people approach and stand at "Ground Zero" in New York City, no one speaks. Within the perimeter of the memorial. a hush buffers the noise and energy of the city. At the Vietnam Memorial in Washington D. C., a father was overheard telling his small child, "Hush, son. This is like church."

In many Protestant churches people enter without signs of reverence. They greet one another, chat with their neighbors, catch-up on the latest news and ball scores until the prelude begins and a modicum of reverence is attained. What has happened to holy ground and reverence in our churches?

One reason there is a dearth of places today considered to be holy ground relates to God's name. Remember, holy name...holy place. For some, God's name is no longer holy. It has lost its mystifying, mysterious cloak of holiness. In the Old Testament God's name was so sacred it could not be uttered. His name was a solemn *Thou.* Once the name of the Lord evoked power. Now, it evokes profane, powerless language. The story of Rumpelstiltskin comes to mind. As long as no one could pronounce the fabled gnome's name, he possessed magical powers. Once his name was uttered, the magical powers vanished.

The Passover and the Exodus

The Passover and the Exodus are to Jews what The Last Supper/Crucifixion and Resurrection are to Christians. They are inextricably bound together and cannot be separated theologically. But for purposes of commentary and meditation they are presented under separate headings.

The Passover

The Passover is a ceremonial feast which commemorates a great moment in the history of the Jewish people, the eve of the beginning of their deliverance from slavery. Other nations and cultures have attempted to connect great moments in their history with a ceremonial meal but the results have been disappointing. These occasions usually degenerate over time into raucous and rowdy celebrations in which the original meaning of the event is lost in the revelry. The Passover has succeeded because of the integration of reminiscences, images and symbols (unleavened bread, bitter herbs, and sacrifice) which evoke powerful thoughts and feelings as if the event were reoccurring.

This same evoking of thought and sentiment passed from Jewish into Christian hands as the Holy Communion. It, too, is a feast filled with powerful symbols (bread, wine, and sacrifice) in the presence of

God's deliverances in the past. Early Christians celebrated the supper at the command of Jesus as a "thanksgiving," or Eucharist from the Greek word *eucharistia* (Matthew 26: 26-29; Mark 14: 22-25; Luke 22:19-22; 1 Corinthians 11:23-26). Because of their rich Jewish heritage, the observance of Holy Communion for Christians possessed the same dynamism as the Passover. When the bread was broken, the wine poured and consumed, Christ was present. The Roman Catholic Church carries this logic to its ultimate conclusion in the transubstantiation of Christ's body and blood, i.e. at the words of the priest, "this is my body," the bread becomes the body of Christ and the wine becomes his blood. We Christians can be thankful to the Jewish faith for passing to us the sense of "reenactment." Each time we break the bread and drink the wine, Christ is present and the Lord's Supper reoccurs.

The spreading of blood over the door of each Hebrew home also found its way into Christian practice. For early Christians, many of whom were Jews, the "blood of the Lamb" signified the offering Christ made of himself on the Cross. John the Baptist called Jesus "The Lamb of God"(John 1:36).

The Exodus

God's call for Moses to become the liberator of his captive people in Egypt is clear and concise: **"So now go. I am sending you to Pharaoh to bring my people the Israelites out of Egypt"** (Ex. 3:10). The confrontation with Pharaoh is the first great task Moses faces. God's demand, "Let my people go" leaves no room for compromise. Moses must press on in that demand until the objective is accomplished. This type of confrontation with evil forces has been repeated in almost every generation. Wherever God's people are being oppressed, God's call, "Let my people go," echoes through history.

Three illustrations of that call to freedom and justice, and the spokesmen that God used to accomplish his purpose in those instances, mark the pages of 20th century history. First was Mahatma Gandhi, the great Indian leader who demanded freedom and justice for his oppressed brothers and sisters in India. Long under British Rule, he was able to lead a successful movement to relieve the yoke of servitude and second-class citizenship for his people. Dr. Martin Luther King, Jr. also fulfilled God's mission by demanding equal rights for African Americans after long years of slavery and segregation. "Let my people go" rang loud and clear in the Civil Rights Movement in the United States. Persecuted, and finally murdered, King lived the life of a prophet and a deliverer, much like Moses. The third parallel experience of a leader being called to demand that his people be freed from oppression was the work of Nelson Mandela of South Africa. Much like the people of India, South African Blacks and Coloreds where accorded very little freedom and faced unspeakable barriers to a better life. Mandela, imprisoned for many years, was finally freed and continued the work that brought about a new day for the people of South Africa. He is still alive at this writing. In all these cases, God used people to stand in the gap and demonstrate an end to oppression. God's justice prevailed, just as it did with Moses in the Exodus.

Two and a half centuries ago, an American Continental Congress sent a message to King George III and the British Parliament to "let our people go." In 1776, the American colonies took heart and courage and declared their independence. On at least two occasions—Brooklyn Heights and the East River; Trenton and the Delaware—occurrences of nature opened paths for Washington's army that later closed on the enemy. The providential flashes may have caused Benjamin Franklin to pen these words:

> Pharaoh sitting in an open chariot, a crown on his head
>
> and a sword in his hand, passing through the divided waters
>
> of the Red Sea in pursuit of the Israelites. Rays from a
>
> pillar of fire in the cloud, expressive of the Divine presence
>
> and command, beaming on Moses, who stands on the shore
>
> and, extending his hand over the sea, causes it to overflow
>
> Pharaoh. Motto: "Rebellion to Tyrants is obedience to
>
> God."[54]

Almost a century after Franklin penned those words, a latter-day Moses rose from the heart of America, one whose life strongly resembles the Exodus leader. By a strange irony of history his first name is Abraham. It is difficult to read the life of Abraham Lincoln and not think of Moses. Both have humble origins and mothers of poverty. Both studied the laws of their religion and country. Both abhorred slavery and its cruelty. Moses saw it first-hand in the brick fields of Egypt, and in New Orleans, Lincoln watched as a mulatto girl was put up for auction. Both freed people from slavery. A parallel can be drawn between the Emancipation Proclamation and the Crossing of the Red Sea. Both ushered in a new era of freedom, a new land of promise. Both died, unable to see their dreams fulfilled.

Throughout this book, one objective has been to show how Old Testament stories, when reinterpreted within a 21st century context, continue to speak today. Another objective has been to show the relevance and linkage of those stories to the New Testament and contemporary Christianity. Nowhere is that linkage more clearly demonstrated than with the Exodus and Passover.

An often over-looked fragment of scripture in the Exodus story occurs immediately prior to the dramatic crossing of the sea, **When the Pharaoh let the people go** (13: 17). Two roads diverged there in that Egyptian dawn. The Israelites must take one. They could take the **road through the Philistine country, though that was shorter,** (13:17b) or they could take the longer route **around by the desert road toward the Red Sea.** (13:18) Scripture reports, they took the desert road to the Red Sea, "the longer road…the one less traveled by and that…made all the difference."[55] The quote from Frost, a parallel of the scripture, is irresistible. Often the longer route God chooses for us, the one across the desert, the one we would not have taken, is the right road for us. The longer, more difficult roads are, in the *long* run, the ones that take us home, to ourselves, to our true identity. Those are the long hard roads that deliver us from captivity, from addiction, from co-dependencies and over-attachments. As with the Israelites, the way God chooses for us is the right way for us.

Do not be afraid, Moses said to the people. **Stand firm and you will see the deliverance the Lord will bring you today** (14:13-14).

This is responsible leadership. This is the confidence of a person of faith. This confidence was reflected in Ghandi facing the British Army; Martin Luther King, Jr. facing police troops and dogs in Selma, Alabama; Rosa Parks refusing to give up her seat on a bus in Montgomery. This is the self-assurance of George Washington after losing New York City; of Abe Lincoln in one of his most trying days when he wrote these words: "Whatever He designs, He will do for me yet. 'Stand still and see the salvation of the Lord' is my text just now."[56] This is Jesus of Nazareth with his disciples in a storm (Mark 4:39-40 and 6: 50, Luke 8:22-25) and his comforting words to them after his resurrection (Matthew 28:10; cf. 1 Peter 5:9, 12).

The crossing of the Red Sea (or Reed Sea, as some scholars theorize) has been controversial. For many in the 21st century, the act of Moses stretching his hand over the sea and the waters dividing to allow the Israelites safe passage on dry land seems incredulous. Equally unbelievable is the reverse movement, his hand goes out and the waters return drowning the Egyptian army. The scene was incredulous in other centuries as well, particularly since the 18th century and the dawn of scientific reason.

The key issue in the story is not the miraculous parting of the waters. Faith is the core message. Did the waters part because Moses raised his hand or did Moses have faith his people would survive? We do not know exactly what happened. Some archaeologists and biblical scholars state no evidence exists suggesting the event occurred. It is not mentioned in Egyptian annals. Other scholars counter the Egyptians would not memorialize a defeat. The historical fact of the event is not at issue. Faith in God brought salvation to Israel is the message, not whether Moses raised his hand and the waters parted. The mechanics of the event are overshadowed by the overarching act of salvation. This is one of those events in history that reminds us of the young boy who, upon seeing the Grand Canyon for the first time, exclaimed, "Mommy, something big happened here."

We are often called to believe the unbelievable. Throughout this book, we have tried to point to the eternal message within the story. The stories have been told so often we grow comfortable with the minor elements, become consumed with the action and forget the major points.

The Exodus story reminds us of God's all-knowing and ultimate power over nature and human life. God's choices can affect many people. Often he sends warnings that are not heeded. When people are stubborn they reap the fairness of God's judgments. The dominant theme of the Red Sea crossing is confidence and faith in God. With God, there are no insurmountable barriers. In the New Testament, Jesus was constantly reminding his listeners, faith creates miracles; miracles do not create faith (Matthew 8:12; Mark 5:34; Luke 8:50).

The story of Moses and the Israelites crossing the Red Sea is a summons to faith. Paul may have been reflecting on the event when he wrote, "No, in all these things we are more than conquerors through him who loved us" (Romans 8:37). With the Red Sea crossing, "The faith to which Israel is here summoned is not a faith the world easily believes and is arrived at by common sense. It is trust against the evidence; risk in the face of the odds, that life can come even in the public domain, where Yahweh governs."[57] Tertullian, the great early church father, once commented of the resurrection of Christ, "It must be believed because it is absurd."[58]

Ten Commandments

The Ten Commandments, handed down from God through Moses, have survived the scrutiny of millennia. Throughout history, these ten "laws' have influenced governments and are responsible for the constitutions and legal structure of many nations.

As noted above, The Ten Commandments, or Decalogue ("Ten Words" in Hebrew), come in two parts. The first four commandments focus on human relations and duties toward God and the remaining six on the relations and duties of humans with each other. The two divisions are summarized in the Old Testament as love to God (Deuteronomy 6:5) and love to neighbor (Leviticus 19:18). Jesus further condensed the commandments: "Love the Lord your God with all your heart and with all your soul and with all your mind. This is the first great commandment. And the second is like it: Love your neighbor as yourself. All the law and the prophets hang on these two commandments" (Matthew 22:37-40. Cf. also Luke 10:27 and Mark 12:30-31).

Consider for a moment what a world without commandments would be? People would create their own rules which could result in anarchy or an absence of rule. An analogy might be playing a football game without sidelines, end zones, referees, or rules. Rules and boundaries, even Death as the ultimate boundary, bring meaning to life.

The number of the commandments is unimportant. Twelve would have been more biblical, more Hebraic. Two is sufficient, all encompassing. We should give thanks daily that we have them, that the writers of ancient biblical texts divinely received them as part and parcel of the order of the divine creation, and as part and parcel of the divinely created *order*. **God said, "Let there be light . . . .** (Genesis 1:3) God spoke and the world came into being. The words came in a certain order and in a certain order the creation developed. The Ten Commandments, or Ten Words, did not originate on Mount Sinai with Moses. They may have been written or chiseled there. But the Ten Commandments, summarized by Jesus as "all the law and the prophets" are best described in the Gospel of John: "In the beginning was the Word, and the Word was with God, and the Word was God" (1:1-2). In other words, the moral order of the universe is as eternal as Father, Son, and Holy Spirit.

With God's moral order comes discipline and with discipline comes freedom. Indeed, St. Paul may have been recalling the words of Jesus but had an Old Testament scroll open to Leviticus 19:18 when he wrote these words: "You, my brothers, were called to be free. But do not use your freedom to indulge the sinful nature, rather serve one another in love. The entire law is summed up in a single command, 'Love your neighbor as yourself'"(Galatians 5: 13-14). And again in Romans, "those who live in accordance with the Spirit have their minds set on what the Spirit desires...the mind controlled by the Spirit is life and peace" (8:5-6; cf. also Romans 8:5ff).

Without God's moral order and without spiritual discipline, there can be no "life and peace." The fathers of our country were in accordance with these principles when they signed a document stating: "We hold these truths to be self-evident, that all men are created equal, that they are endowed by their Creator with certain unalienable Rights, that among these are Life, Liberty, and the pursuit of Happiness."

They were well aware of the Ten Commandments and the inseparableness of God's moral order and human liberty.

In conclusion, the Ten Commandments occupy a fundamental position in the Judeo-Christian faith. Christians as well as Jews hold these Ten Commandments as God-given and non-negotiable. They were not "suggestions," but commandments. They were the constitutional law of ancient Israel and became the absolute ethical norm for the Jewish community.

The Ten Commandments were important to Jesus and acknowledged by him. Though he does not quote them all, Jesus does references several (Matthew 19:16-22; Mark 10:17-22 and Luke 18:18-30). He said, "Do not think that I have come to abolish the Law and the Prophets; I have not come to abolish them but to fulfill them"(Mt. 5:17). When asked which is the greatest commandment, Jesus answered, "Love the Lord your God with all your heart and with all your soul and with all your mind. This is the first and greatest commandment. And the second is like unto it: 'Love your neighbor as yourself'. All the Law and the Prophets hang on these two commandments" (Mt. 22:37-40).

The New Interpreter's Bible comments that, "the commandments are, for Jesus, a first-level demand, preparatory to the more rigorous demand, 'go, sell, give, come, follow.' In these narratives, the commands are not considered unattainable modes of conduct; they are, rather, the threshold to more serious discipleship and a step on the demanding way to 'eternal life.'"[59]

Due to their strong linkage with Moses and importance to the Old Testament, The Message of the Ten Commandments is presented below as a separate segment.

The Ten Commandments

THE MESSAGE

In the beginning God created the heavens and the earth (Genesis 1:1). The Ten Commandments begin, **You shall have no other gods before me.** (20:3).What if there was not just one God, but many gods. What kind of moral/ethical confusion would that present? Which god would we follow? In the days of the early church, a heretic named Basilides adopted 365 gods, one for every day of the year. Since these gods all had different rules, regulations, rituals, ceremonies, laws, *ad naseum*, religious anarchy reigned. Individuals following Basilides had some form of worshiper's almanac and knew which gods to worship on each calendar day. Granted, there was a sense of order. But it was day to day. There was no consistency. Each day a different god was in charge. What would happen if each day a different President of the U.S.A. were in charge? There are times, we wonder, if that is not the case. There would be chaos. In religion, having more than one god results in ethical and moral fragmentation, diffusion and confusion of beliefs, psychological split and disintegration, loss of personal (and often cultural and national) identity, and an overall general societal malaise. This chaos was the state of the Roman Empire when Jesus of Nazareth appeared and this was a major reason his message resonated. In response to a question from the crowd, "'Of all the commandments, which is the most important?' 'The most important one,' answered Jesus, 'is this, Hear, O Israel, the Lord our God, the Lord is one. Love the Lord your God with all your heart and with all your soul and with all your strength'" (Mark 12:28-30).

The Jews did worship one God, but their God had become relegated to the Temple, veiled in the Holy of Holies. This was not the same God of Abraham, Isaac, and Jacob. Filtered through centuries of legal tradition, this God had morphed into something different. The First Commandment, in the eyes of Jesus, had been broken by his own people. They had confined the vibrant God of their heritage to cold storage in the Temple. Jesus' message was simple and back to basics: "Hear, O Israel, the Lord our God, the Lord is one." He knew, too, the futility of having more than one god: "No man can serve two masters. Either he will hate the one and love the other, or he will be devoted to the one and despise the other. You cannot serve both God and Money" (Matthew 6:24). An alternate translation is: You can serve only one God. "No one is good except God Alone" (Mark 10:18)

You shall not make for yourselves an idol... (20:4)[60]

From the pulpit, church school curriculum, and pop-religion we often hear or read of "the other gods" we serve. To identify those "other gods," pastors encourage us to review our check stubs. The technique is overused, especially during stewardship drives, but it is not without validity. Jesus used a similar approach with the Rich Young Ruler. (Matthew 19:16-22; Mark 10:17-23, and Luke 18:18-23) All three gospel writers tell the story with the major focus upon worshiping the one God and keeping His commandments.

In a study group recently, someone asked the question, "Is worshipping one God practical?" At first, the question seemed "off the wall." Yet, in our capitalistic driven economic age, the question implied that worshipping more than one god, possibly several, might be more practical. Based upon issues raised in the previous paragraph, we do "worship" several gods. The question on its merits deserves an answer.

In ancient and modern times some economies depend on polytheism, or the worship of many gods. Given the high level of commercialism in "the Holy Land," some economies thrive on the worship of one God. Religion, of any kind, can be good for business. It can also be bad. St. Paul caused riots with his sermons about worshiping one God. The artisans and craftsmen of Ephesus who sold idols and sacrifices for the pagan temples, particularly for the god Artemis, went on a rampage. "He says that man-made gods are not gods at all," they said of Paul. His one God hit their pocketbooks. John Wesley created similar outrages in England with his sermons against rum, ale, and pub life.

Spiritual issues and dogma aside, worshipping one God can be very practical. Ecclesiastes states, "…money is the answer for everything," (10:19b) but Jesus poses the dilemma, "You cannot serve both God and Money" (Matthew 6:24b; Luke 16:13b). Jesus creates an interesting twist with the two concepts. If you keep the first commandment and second commandments, bring your budget into accord with their spiritual values, you will significantly reduce spending on items other than necessities. This strategy would also increase the amount you could give to your church and to charities.

Believing in one God is also practical from a psychological perspective. Sound psychological health rests upon a foundation of a sound integrated personality, or "wholeness," the origin of the word "holy." Holistic health has its origins in the ancient wisdom of harmony of mind, body, emotions, and spirit. The human personality cannot be neatly segmented into physical, mental, emotional, or spiritual. All components were designed by the Creator to work as an integrated whole. Spirituality is one of those components. Believing in, and worshiping, one God is spiritual integrity and wholeness.

Spirituality is based upon belief systems which involves feelings. The more focused one's feelings and thoughts, the more focused is their spiritual self. If that focus is divided, the result is confusion at other layers of thought. Danish Theologian Søren Kierkegaard presents this principle beautifully in his book *Purity of Heart Is To Will One Thing.*[61] Belief in more than one god creates a higher level of divided values and cognitive dissonance which in turn fuels anxiety. We would paraphrase Kierkegaard and say, "Emotional well-being is to believe in one God."

You shall not misuse the name of the Lord your God is the *NIV* translation of the more familiar *King James Version,* "Thou shalt not take the name of the Lord in vain" (20:7). The third commandment relates more to the issue of God's character as beyond influence and control rather than profanity as we understand "misuse" or "in vain" today. The commandment applies a much broader interpretation and casts a wider net. Any misuse of God's name, not just cursing, is forbidden.

Using someone else's name is easy. In order to gain a favor, obtain a promotion, win a scholarship, make a sale, have you ever used someone's name without their permission? Today, theft of another's identity is commonplace. Millions know the feeling of having their social security or credit card numbers stolen. How would you feel if someone else hijacked your name? What label would you apply to that feeling? "Robbed," "cheated," "exploited," "used," are words that come to mind. No one but God knows His emotions. Yet, if we are made in his image and likeness, we might have an inkling how he feels when his name is misused, when His sacred and hallowed identity is profaned. One of the greatest books on this subject is Martin Buber's *I and Thou.*[62] In this famous work, the Jewish theologian proposes that all human relationships emerge ultimately into a relationship with God, the everlasting Thou. Within this context, anytime we misuse the name or identity of another human being, we are, in essence, breaching the third commandment. We are treating them as an "it" and not a "thou." We are not in relationship, but controlling. "So, when Jesus says 'Love thy neighbor as thyself,' he is saying in effect. "Love thy neighbor because he is thyself.""[63]

God is beyond human control. Conversion decisions are between God, who initiates the decision freely through His grace, and the believer. Though strong preaching, stirring hymns, and emotional worship services may be present an atmosphere for conversion, those elements are mere background. Based on the scripture as translated, the Lord's name is misused when anyone manipulates and/or takes credit for the spiritual decision of another. We are influenced by certain events, scenarios, drama, music, oratory, etc., but in spiritual matters, God is completely in control.

The first three commandments rise and fall together. One cannot exist without the other two. They form an inter-dependent composite, an early Trinitarian formula, defining the nature of God and human relationship to him.

Remember the Sabbath day by keeping it holy. The argument is made that the fourth commandment is intertwined with the first three. The key word is "holy." As expressed several times, the word holy in its early Judeo-Christian usage meant a healthy, wholesome integrated personality. God rested and refreshed on the seventh day. He expects the same of his creatures. The scripture is very specific: " . . . the seventh day is a Sabbath to the Lord your God" (20:10). The foundation for the command comes from the creation story, Genesis 1:1-2:4a. Regardless of its origin, (probably during the Exile with circumcision as a mark of Judaism), the Sabbath was absorbed with equal sacredness into the Christian faith. The theme is *rest*, not a particular *day*, as Jesus noted in some of his statements. (Matthew 10:11-12; Mark 2:27; Luke 13:15-16; Luke 6:3-5; John: 16-17) Within this context, taking a Sabbath can mean breaking stressful unhealthy patterns of behavior and creating new patterns of health healing. Again, the key word is "holy." On a concluding note, for all nature lovers, animals had a special status on the Sabbath.

The fifth commandment promotes the integrity of the family unit. Another emphasis, noted in the Exegesis, links to the passage of land from family to family. But the primary intent of the commandment is to protect the elderly and providing security and opportunity for longevity.

Honor for the elderly is a value still held in high regard in Asian countries. But the values of the West, where youth is worshipped and old age dreaded or despised, are far removed from adoration and worship of the elderly. "Honor your father and your mother" also implies, "Honor your own aging process." We tend to think of aging as subtracting from our lives rather than adding. Psychological research notes that in several cognitive categories, older people are smarter. They lose ground on those tests which measure response time.

Are we seventy years young or seventy years old? The numbers are unimportant. As we age, our essence is undiminished. The same is true of our parents. Proudly, and reverentially, we should honor them, and particularly as they grow older.

You shall not murder establishes the sacredness and God's sovereignty over human life. Killing another person is prohibited. Joseph Campbell notes, " . . . the ten commandments say 'thou shalt not kill.' Then the next chapter says, "Go into Canaan and kill everybody in it."[64] This and other apparent contradictions in the Old Testament are reminders that any interpretation of this commandment must move beyond the patriarchal confines of its historical context and into the 21st century world of values. Right to Life and Capital Punishment are hot political buttons in our time. Are the positions as inconsistent as the scriptures cited above? Many who support the Right to Life platform, which presumes the sacredness of life, are strongly in favor of the death penalty. The contradiction is a reminder that all life is of God and all life is sacred.

Problems with the death penalty are numerous. Innocent people have been wrongly convicted and executed. Trial by jury is a human, not a divine, process. Humans err. Research conducted several years ago by the National Jury Project, suggested seventy-five (75) percent of potential jurors lie during *voir dire* (a French phrase meaning "truth talk") when the attorneys and judge ask them questions about their background and personal feelings.[65] Capital crime trials are flawed from the beginning. As Christians, we believe in the forgiveness of sins and spiritual regeneration. Rehabilitation is a Christian value. The death penalty is also economically impracticable. The required appeal of a single death penalty verdict costs states hundreds of thousands of dollars. A life sentence without parole costs less than fifty dollars per day. Criminals can be rehabilitated behind prison walls and make contributions to society while incarcerated. In his persecution of Christians, which included the death of Stephen, St. Paul might be classified a murderer. Where would the Christian Church be today if he had been executed, his conversion and confession discounted? This commandment must be interpreted within the context of the New Testament and life of Jesus. You shall not take the life of another, regardless.

How does **You shall not murder** apply to war? In the Old Testament the commandment permitted taking the life of the enemy. In Christianity, the three primary positions on war are the crusade, the just war, and pacifism. The crusade is prominent in the Old Testament. Pacifism dominates the New Testament. The concept of the "just war" is of more recent origins and evolved primarily from the Viet Nam era. Among the criteria of a just war are the following: (1) a just war must be a last resort waged by a legitimate authority, (2) it must redress a wrong which has been inflicted and suffered, (3) there must be a reasonable chance of success, (4) peace must be the ultimate goal, (5) the violence used in the war must be commensurate with the wrong inflicted, (6) the weapons must discriminate between combatants and non-combatants. Our readers must decide if killing and war can be justified. The answer to three questions might prove helpful: Does God justify killing? Does Christ justify killing? Does the Holy Spirit justify killing?

Jesus acknowledged all of the commandments: "Do not think that I have come to abolish the Law or the Prophets; I have not come to abolish them but to fulfill them" (Matthew 5:17). His idea of fulfillment tightened the law and left none without sin. This was particularly true of several commandments, the sixth included: "You have heard that it was said to the people long ago, 'Do not murder, and anyone who murders will be subject to judgment.' But I tell you that anyone who is angry with his brother will be subject to judgment" (Matthew 5:21-22) Jesus' idea of fulfilling the law is reflected in Gilbert Keith Chesterton's statement, "Christianity, even when watered down, is hot enough to boil all of society to rags."[66]

Since both embrace family integrity, **You shall not commit adultery** (20:14) should follow **Honor your father and your mother.** (20:12) But adultery is categorized as a form of theft and therefore grouped with the last three commandments. Others theorize an ancient scribe missed a line and copied the commandment out of sequence. Though one might argue that keeping the fifth would prevent breaking the seventh, the ranking of the commandments is inconsequential. All share equal importance.

The commandment prohibiting adultery upholds the sanctity of marriage, the spiritual ties that bind the relationship, and the strong warning against physical appetites and desires assailing that sacred bond. Originally, the commandment reflected the male perspective with an interpretation of wife as property. Over time the meaning has applied to both husband and wife. Joseph Campbell puts the partnership in perspective: "Marriage is a relationship. When you make the sacrifice in marriage, you're sacrificing not to each other but to unity in a relationship . . . . Marriage is not a simple love affair, it is an ordeal, and the ordeal is the sacrifice of the ego to a relationship . . . . "[67]

Adultery is a hurtful sacrifice. The welfare of a family unit, the happiness of children, the feelings of countless others within the extended network are sacrificed on the altar of immediate need gratification.

Marriage is complicated and complex. At times there are issues of abuse, extenuating circumstances no one would really understand except those involved. Options are varied and equally complex, but, according to the Old and the New Testament, adultery is not one of them. Jesus' comments about the commandment included everyone: "You have heard that it was said, "Do not commit adultery.' But I tell you that anyone who looks at a woman lustfully has already committed adultery with her in his heart" (Matthew 5:27-28).

You shall not steal. (20:15) "Now, no matter what the mullah teaches, there is only one sin, only one. And that is theft. Do you understand that? . . . ." When you kill a man you steal a life," Baba said. "You steal his wife's right to a husband, rob his children of a father. When you tell a lie, you steal someone's right to the truth. When you cheat, you steal the right to fairness. Do you see?"[68] This comment from Khaled Hosseini's best-selling novel, *The Kite Runner,* describes some of the many ways of theft. Not included are the earlier commandments related to God's sovereignty and misuse of his name or how we steal another's name when we use it without permission. There are other facets of theft. Am I robbing someone when I raise my prices far above the market price? Is price-gouging a form of theft? If I sell a product without all the parts advertised, do I not steal from my customer? When we tell a lie, do we steal the truth? When asked how his father became a British Lord, a young college student responded, "Because his great-great grandfather started stealing before everyone else did." Theft is a wide net.

On a larger scale, the issue of theft must be addressed among states and nations, particularly between wealthy developed economies and the poverty of third world nations. When large, powerful nations conquer small, defenseless nations, greed motivates theft and all of humankind is affected. This statement from the Exegesis is worth re-stating: "Theft of another, of anything, is a breach of the covenant of the community. To steal from one, is to steal from all."

You shall not give false testimony against your neighbor. (20:16)

The ninth commandment related primarily to legal testimony and insured the sacredness of the judicial system. As noted above, seventy-five percent of potential jurors lie when asked qualifying questions in court. A law on the books is no guarantee the truth will be told.

This commandment originally carried a legal meaning but it basically says, "Don't tell lies about people." The Old Testament placed a high premium upon the truth (Deuteronomy 13:14; 17:4; 22:20; Jeremiah 9:5; Psalms 15:2; Proverbs 12:19; 14:25; 22:21). Telling a lie about another is a form of theft. Their identity and status in the community is diminished, in some cases obliterated. Sadly, the perpetrators of false testimony steal from themselves. Their core identity is weakened. Over time, self-concept, self-confidence, and self-esteem can become obliterated. The bearers of false testimony steal themselves blind. Usually, people tell falsehoods on others to make themselves look better. In reality, the opposite occurs.

On any given news day someone commits perjury. In local, national, and international headlines, people lie to police, to lawyers, and to judges and juries. They cover up, stonewall, deceive, evade, and skirt the truth. Consider a world with no commandment against lying about one's neighbor. Ponder for a moment the state of your community if anyone could say anything about anyone and there were no laws to protect the innocent. The ancient Israelites, and the Babylonians before them, considered that chaotic scenario and forged a commandment giving integrity and clout to their judicial system.

Often we lie to others unintentionally. We say nice things because we do not want to, "hurt their feelings." This is a form of emotional dishonesty called "passive behavior." Passive behavior not only undermines relationships, it is the perfect strategy for depression. When people are not emotionally honesty, they sacrifice personal integrity. They give up a part of themselves. Over time, nothing is left. They have no identity. Passive behavior is also a subtle form of selfishness. Why do we not want to say anything that will upset another? We want them to "like" us. Jesus of Nazareth was loving and caring; he was also direct and straight-forward, emotionally honest to a fault, and to a cross.

You shall not covet . . . . The clear intent of this commandment is to prohibit thoughts which would lead to actual deeds of theft, adultery, and murder. This commandment is an acknowledgement by the ancients that the breeding place of sinful acts is within the person. One's destiny is determined not by their gallantry and heroism but by purity of heart. Jesus underscored this concept. With its focus on the inward thought, this commandment may well be the threshold of the New Testament. Jesus was keenly aware of that downward slope and encouraged his followers to covet righteousness (Matthew 5:6).

Covetousness today is reflected in unbridled consumerism in which we accumulate material things to match our neighbor's accumulation. The behavior is called "keeping up with the Joneses." Much of this attitude stems from our emphasis upon individualism and the focus on self and satisfying the needs of self. It also teaches the false assumption that we can have anything we want. Psychologically, this kind of behavior is unhealthy. Instead of establishing identity, the opposite occurs. One's sense of self is displaced with ownership of "things."

The tenth commandment is the appropriate conclusion to the Decalogue and brings us full cycle: **You shall have no other gods before me.** The first and tenth commandments bracket the others and demonstrate how the Ten Commandments function as a unitary whole. They are all inter-related, each to the whole and to each other. Coveting means having other gods, thus keeping the first commandment helps protect the sanctity of the tenth. Violating the tenth commandment means violating the first. Another example relates to the fourth commandment. Keeping the Sabbath supports the first three commandments and serves as deterrence to the remaining six. Sabbath keeping prevents the types of activity and energy that tempt or cause violation of the others. *The HarperCollins Bible Dictionary* compares the Ten Commandments to ten posts supporting the fence dividing Israel from the rest of the pagan world: "Should any of these ten fence posts collapse, chaos could break in and wreak havoc in the community. For Israel survival was at stake with every one of these ten categorical imperatives."[69]

Conclusion

The Ten Commandments occupy a fundamental position in the Judeo-Christian faith. Christians as well as Jews hold these Ten Commandments as God-given and non-negotiable. They were not "suggestions," but commandments. They were the constitutional law of ancient Israel and became the absolute ethical norm for the Jewish community.

The Ten Commandments were important to Jesus and acknowledged by him. Though he does not quote them all, Jesus references several (Matthew 19:16-22; Mark 10:17-22 and Luke 18:18-30). He said, "Do not think that I have come to abolish the Law and the Prophets; I have not come to abolish them but to fulfill them" (Mt. 5:17). When asked to cite the greatest commandment, Jesus answered, "Love the Lord your God with all your heart and with all your soul and with all your mind. This is the first and greatest commandment. And the second is like unto it: 'Love your neighbor as yourself'. All the Law and the Prophets hang on these two commandments" (Mt. 22:37-40).

The New Interpreter's Bible comments that, "the commandments are, for Jesus, a first-level demand, preparatory to the more rigorous demand, 'go, sell, give, come, follow.' In these narratives, the commands are not considered unattainable modes of conduct; they are, rather, the threshold to more serious discipleship and a step on the demanding way to 'eternal life.'"[70]

QUESTIONS FOR FURTHER STUDY AND DISCUSSION

1. What is the importance of the Exodus to the history of the People of Israel?

2. An Epiphany is the appearance or manifestation of a god or other supernatural being. What was the significance of Moses' Epiphany and a bush that was burning but not consumed? Have you ever experienced an Epiphany? If so, how has it affected your life?

3. Where are the places you consider "Holy Ground"? What makes a place "Holy Ground"?

4. What experiences can you recall where/when you felt you were in the living presence of God? What were your feelings and sensations? Do you remember the locations? Today, do you consider them "holy" places?

5. What does it mean to be called by God? Have you ever felt that you were receiving a divine message to accomplish something special?

6. What is your understanding of God as "I AM"? How does this characterization of God relate to Jesus' use of the term "I am" found especially in the Gospel of John?

7. Why does Moses hide his face in the presence of God?

8. Why is the Passover such a significant event for faithful Jews? What is the relation of "The Last Supper" to Passover?

9. What are some celebrations/observances in the USA that remind us of special times in our history as a nation?

10. Can you think of ways other than those mentioned in the Commentary of how we misuse, abuse, and manipulate the name of the Lord?

11. What did Jesus mean when he said he had not come to abolish the Law and the Prophets but to fulfill them? (Mt. 5:17) Are Christians still bound by these Commandments?

Chapter Seven

Ruth

THE TEXT

In the days when the judges ruled, there was a famine in the land, and a man from Bethlehem in Judah, together with his wife and two sons, went to live for a while in the country of Moab . . . . After they had lived there about ten years . . . . Naomi was left without her two sons and her husband . . . .

—Ruth 1:1-5

Then Naomi said to her two daughters-in-law, "Go back , each of you to your mother's home . . . . But Ruth replied, "Don't urge me to leave you or to turn back from you. Where you go I will go and where you stay I will stay. Your people will be my people and your God my God. Where you die I will die, and there I will be buried . . . . "

—Ruth 1:8, 16-17

Now Naomi had a relative on her husband's side . . . whose name was Boaz.

So Boaz said to Ruth, "My daughter, listen to me . . . stay here with my servant girls . . . I have told the men not to touch you . . . .

At this she bowed down with her face to the ground. She exclaimed, "Why have I found such favor in your eyes that you notice me, a foreigner?"

"I have been told all about what you have done for your mother-in-law since the death of your husband . . . . May the Lord repay you for what you have done . . . .

—Ruth 2:8-12

Then Ruth told her mother-in-law about the one at whose place she had been working . . . . "The Lord bless him," Naomi said to her daughter-in-law . . . that man is our close relative, he is one of our kinsmen-redeemers . . . . "

—Ruth 2:19-20

So Boaz took Ruth and she became his wife. Then he went to her and the Lord enabled her to conceive, and she gave birth to a son...Then Naomi took the child, laid him in her lap and cared for him. The women living there said, "Naomi has a son." And they named him Obed. He was the father of Jesse, the father of David.

—Ruth 4:13, 16-17

THE CONTEXT

The Book of Ruth is the story of Ruth and Naomi, an account of human compassion and loyalty that extends beyond national- or self-interests. It is a classic short story with pathos, humor, romance, intrigue, benevolence and a sharp rebuke against any form of narrow exclusionism. With Jewish emphasis on purity of blood and correctness of genealogy, Ruth was somehow accepted into the canon.

One reason may be the connection with King David. Ruth is a Moabite and becomes King David's great-grandmother, which gives her a prominent place in David's lineage as a forbear of Jesus.

The eighth book of the Old Testament, Ruth is only four chapters long. In the *Tanakh,* Hebrew Bible, it is placed between Lamentations and Song of Songs,[71] In the Christian Old Testament, Ruth follows Judges and precedes 1 Samuel, thus bridging the time of the judges and the beginning of the monarchy. *The New Interpreter's Bible* states, "the way Ruth begins with a reference to the judges and ends with a reference to David informs the reader in advance that the episodes in Samuel dealing with Saul are little more than a detour on the road to the dynasty that really matters, the Davidic line of kings."[72]

The composition of Ruth cannot be dated with certainty. Some scholars contend it was written in the 9th century or in the 5th century BCE. Some believe Ruth was written during the time of David as an attempt to support his monarchy, while others argue it was written after the Babylonian exile to establish the legitimacy of the Messiah. "The excellent classical style of the book, and the use of a number of archaic verbal forms, are entirely appropriate to this earliest period of Hebrew literature. In its present form, however, the book of Ruth shows considerable evidence of a postexilic date, i.e., sometime between 450 and 250 BCE."[73] The linguistic evidence is too vague, ambiguous and confusing to allow for an accurate estimate of the time of composition. Authorship is also unknown. "According to the tradition of the Talmud (B.B. 14b), Samuel was the author of Judges and Ruth, as well as of the book that bears his name."[74]

The book of Ruth must be appreciated and understood as an entertaining narrative *story,* similar in form and function to the Book of Jonah. It also resembles stories in Genesis 22, 24, and 38; the Joseph series; Job (1; 42:7-17); and episodes in 2 Samuel 9-20. It was probably passed orally through generations as one of the great stories of Israel's early history. The narrative is compact and well-written, a short story about the lives of ordinary people, their problems, and the issues of their time. It can be read as a drama in four acts with a prologue and epilogue attached. Some consider Ruth to be a lengthy parable without historical or political elements. The story unfolds through conversations grouped around six scenes and, according to some scholars, is a seamless piece with no indications of additions, edits or redactions.[75]

The Story

In the days of the Judges a famine occurred in the land and an Israelite family from Bethlehem—Elimelech, his wife Namoi and their two sons Mahlon and Chilion—immigrate to the adjacent country of Moab. Elimelech dies and his two sons marry Moabite women. Mahlon marries Ruth and Chilion marries Orpah. Later, Elimelech's sons die. The widow, Naomi, must decide whether to remain in Moab or return to her home in Bethlehem. She decides to go home to Bethlehem and instructs her daughters-in-law, who are also widows, to return to their homes and mothers, and seek to remarry.

Reluctantly, Orpha returns to her home, but Ruth remains with Naomi: **Don't urge me to leave you or to turn back from you. Where you go I will go, and where you stay I will stay. Your people will be my people and your God my God. Where you die I will die, and there I will be buried. May the Lord deal with me, be it ever so severely, if anything but death separates you and me.** (1:16-17)

Naomi and Ruth return to Jerusalem during the season of the barley harvest. To support them, Ruth works in the barley fields owned by Boaz, a well-to-do landowner in Bethlehem. Boaz is kind to Ruth. He is impressed with her loyalty to her mother-in-law. For the remainder of the barley harvest season, Ruth works in Boaz's fields.

Boaz is closely related to the family of Naomi's husband. According to the *levirate* law, Boaz is obligated to marry Mahlon's widow, Ruth, in order to maintain his family's ancestral line. At Naomi's instruction, Ruth goes to the threshing floor each evening and uncovers the feet of Boaz as he sleeps. Ruth does as Naomi tells her, and when Boaz awakens, she reminds him he is **a kinsman-redeemer.** (3:9b) Boaz agrees to "redeem" Ruth, but he tells her another relative has stronger rights. The following morning, Boaz confers with this man in the company of the town elders. The other man fears his marriage to Ruth might jeopardize the inheritance of his own estate and he rejects the offer.

Boaz and Ruth marry and have a son, Obed. According to levirate customs, Obed is also considered an heir to Mahlon and, therefore, Naomi's grandson. In the genealogy at the end of the story, Obed is distinguished as a descendant of Perez, the son of Judah. As the father of Jesse, Obed becomes the grandfather of David.

THE MESSAGE

Ezra and Nehemiah had instituted strict rules regarding the marriage of Jewish men to foreign women. In 458, Ezra, a priest, led a group of exiles from Babylon back to Jerusalem. Nehemiah had returned earlier and supervised the rebuilding of the Walls around Jerusalem. Nehemiah served as governor of Judea, 444-432 BCE. The two leaders collaborated in using text that were found in the rebuilding process to re-codify the laws and added strict laws against intermarriage of Jewish men and non-Jewish women.

The ancient scholars who determined the makeup of the "The Scriptures," were men of vision. The inherent problems in an exclusive race were an elitist religion and nation based upon purity of blood. Even if an exclusive race was possible, it was un-God like. God's love is not exclusive or elitist or based upon privileged or genetic inheritance. God's love is for all regardless of race, nationality, creed, gender, or philosophy. This is Ruth's poignant spiritual message that is echoed in Jonah (Chapter Ten).

The issue of "outsiders" troubled many religious and secular communities of that era and is prominent today in the foreign policy of this and other countries. History is filled with sad illustrations of the violence and exclusion of one people against another. The obvious example was Hitler's attempt to exterminate the Jews in World War II. Related to that holocaust was the Palestinian exodus following the 1948 Arab-Israeli War. In that conflict over 700,000 Arab Palestinians were forced or encouraged to leave their homes and are now the millions of homeless Palestinian refugees living in camps around the

Near East. Palestinian population trends have become a volatile issue in Israel.

In America, the centuries of conflict between white and black races in the South are well documented. This history of exclusion continues with our current debate over immigration. During the Great Depression, fears of nativism and a "Mexican takeover" caused the Great Repatriation in which approximately sixty percent of Mexican-Americans were hastily deported from the Southwestern U. S. to Mexico, many with ancestry dating back to the 19th century.

"Ethnic cleansings"[76] or genocide, the more severe term, are crimes under international law. Both have involved violence against Christians in India, Croats against Bosnian Serbs, Serbs against Bosnian Muslims. Immigrations of Non-Europeans to Britain have created friction within that country. The recent outbreaks in the nation of Georgia stem from the South Ossetia War in which 100,000 ethnic Ossetians fled South Ossetia and Georgia proper across the border into North Ossetia. Recent happenings include the 1994 massacres of nearly a million Tutsis by Hutus, known as Rwanda. White farmers were expelled by the Mugabe regime in Zimbabwe in 2000. In the current Iraqi civil war, entire neighborhoods in Baghdad are being ethnically cleansed by Shi'ite and Sunni Militias. Iraqi Christians, about five percent of the population, comprise forty percent of refugees living in surrounding countries. Ironically, today Bethlehem, the town of Naomi's origin, is isolated by a wall from the remainder of Palestine. Sadly, these issues are unending.

These companion issues of exclusion and purity fill the Old Testament. Ancient sages and prophets decided something should be said. Theologically, the story of Ruth suggests that human action is important in challenging social systems. God may be the "motivator" behind these human actions, but human action is required in changing unjust social systems. Humans are not "puppets" of God.

Opinions differ, however, over why the book was written. Some believe it was intended to tell a story of simple people in the early days of the Hebrews. Though a major theme of the book is incompatible with racial or religious elitism or restriction, the author does not appear to take aim on these issues.

The arguments against pure blood lines and exclusion are only part of the story. Love, loyalty and kindness as pathways to happiness are doubtless key spiritual themes of the book. Ruth's devotion to Naomi, who had lost her husband and two sons, and her insistence on returning with Naomi to her people, is a centerpiece of the story's pathos reflected in the familiar and powerful lines, **"Where you go I will go, and where you stay I will stay. Your people will be my people and your God my God. Where you die I will die, and there I will be buried."** (1:16-17) This statement, **"**has long been taken as a symbol of true friendship between women, parallel to the famous example of the friendship of David and Jonathan. Here is not simply the loyal devotion to a husband which might be expected from a wife, but devotion to a woman who was both a foreigner and a mother-in-law, beyond any reasonable requirement of duty."[77] The care manifested by Ruth is magnified when we consider her parents were probably still alive. (2:11) With her marriage to Boaz, Ruth is a testament that love can cross blood lines, but she teaches the same lesson by treating Naomi more like a mother than a mother-in-law.

Love, loyalty and kindness are part of the Ruth and Boaz story. The nature of their relationship and Ruth's relationship with Naomi reaffirm that God is a God of love of all people. The Jews had a covenantal relationship with God. They were God's chosen people. But where did foreigners stand with them? The story of Ruth and Boaz answers that question. The Danish theologian Søren Kierkegaard wrote a book entitled *Purity Of Heart Is To Will One Thing*. Ruth is exemplary of that single-minded loyalty and fidelity. She had no intentions or expectations, no concept of secondary gains, yet she is richly rewarded.

Ruth was a foreigner but she accepted Israel's God. How many of us could do the same in a Muslim country? Ruth was also a compassionate, caring and accepting person. Without hesitation Boaz married Ruth. Her character eclipsed her natural origin. God blessed this foreigner and used her to become the ancestress of David. The spiritual lesson of this story is that we are called upon to be loyal, loving and caring to all people regardless of their race, ancestry, or religion. We must accept and value these qualities in people who are different from us.

The heroine of this story may be Naomi, not Ruth. Naomi initiates unselfish love by encouraging Ruth to return to her home. When Ruth makes her decision to go with Naomi, she is the one who finds a home for Ruth where she will be well provided.(3:1) Naomi choreographs the romance between Ruth and Boaz. With an element of humor, the writer injects how Naomi schools Ruth in "how to catch a man."(3:1-6) Naomi, experienced in the ways of her people, advises Ruth how to attract Boaz, the kinsman who had given Ruth "gleaning" privileges on his farm. The Book of Ruth contains only 85 verses and uses the word *redeem* 23 times, mostly in association with Ruth. Yet in the end, Naomi is the one redeemed. In fairness, and balance to her character, Naomi resorts to the human emotion of bitterness by blaming God for her problems.

Some relevant issues emerge from the stories within the story. For example, Naomi was a widow. She had also lost both sons. When a man dies today, what is the source of income for his widow? Immediately, we say life insurance, Social Security, pension benefits, her own employment, etc. But are these enough? The loss of the major source of income can be difficult for the spouse, male or female. Reflect on Naomi's loss and how her income was significantly reduced. Boaz demonstrated courage in his invitation to Ruth. The equivalent of that behavior today would be Christians inviting Muslims to a social gathering, evangelicals sitting down with liberals, a wealthy family inviting poor Hispanic immigrants into their home.

The writer of Ruth shows that God's actions and intentions are reflected in human relationships and acts of kindness that go beyond conventional duty. Ruth's love for Naomi, Naomi's love for Ruth, and the love of Ruth and Boaz for each other reveals a pattern of God's love that transcends race and clan. A theme of "redemption" can also be seen in the intriguing story. Boaz becomes Ruth's redeemer, a role that he graciously assumed. This points to the redemptive work of God, finally expressed in the coming of Jesus Christ, God's only son.

QUESTIONS FOR FURTHER STUDY AND DISCUSSION:

1. Why is the story of Ruth important enough to have been included in the Old Testament Canon?
2. What is the main theme of Ruth? How is it relevant to the 21st century?
3. What is the spiritual message in Ruth and Boaz's life?
4. What is important in the birth to the Messiah: a royal line of blood kinship, or a history of lovingkindness, not ethnic purity?
5. If this story was used by Jews opposed to the strict marriage laws instituted by the reforms (re-codification of the Law) by Ezra and Nehemiah, what effect if any did it have?
6. Ruth's love and loyalty for Naomi are legendary. How did Naomi earn devotion from a daughter-in-law?
7. What does this story tell us about the importance of love and loyalty?
8. What other lessons could we learn from the story? About how we treat the poor among us? About generosity to kinfolk who are having hard times? About family solidarity?

Chapter Eight

David: Shepherd King and Messianic Model

Before exploring this chapter, the reader should read the entire books of 1 and 2 Samuel, 1 and 2 Kings, and 1 and 2 Chronicles. That is a large block of material, a tall order. But knowing and understanding the history of the Jewish monarchy is essential to comprehending the role of David in the development of the messianic concept and its relationship to the New Testament and Jesus of Nazareth. Understanding the different points of view reflected by the various writers who compiled these books is equally important. Many first-time readers are confused by the different slants, inconsistencies, and contradictions within the same stories. Do not let those disturb you. Hopefully, the background, exegesis, and commentary of this book will be enlightening. Read the books initially for personal enjoyment and the historic thread of the monarchy.

THE TEXT

The Anointment of David—1 Samuel 16:1-15

Then he consecrated Jesse and his sons and invited them to the sacrifice. When they arrived, Samuel saw Eliba and thought, "Surely the Lord's anointed stands here before the Lord."

But the Lord said to Samuel, "Do not consider his appearance or his height, for I have rejected him. The Lord does not look at the things man looks at. Man looks at the outward appearance, but the Lord looks at the heart."

—1 Samuel 16:5b-7

"There is still the youngest," Jesse answered, "but he is tending the sheep..

Samuel said, "Send for him; we will not sit down until he arrives."

So he sent and had him brought in. He was ruddy, with a fine appearance and handsome features. Then the Lord said, "Rise and anoint him; he is the one."

—1 Sam. 16:11b-12

The Shepherd Warrior and Goliath—1 Samuel 17:1-58

A champion named Goliath, who was from Gath, came out of the Philistine camp. He was over nine feet tall...Goliath stood and shouted to the ranks of Israel . . . . "Choose a man and have him come down to me. If he is able to fight and kill me, we will become your subjects; but if I overcome him and kill him, you will become our subjects and serve us." (1 Sam. 17:4, 8-9)

David said to Saul, "Let no one lose heart on account of this Philistine; your   servant will go and fight him . . . . Then he took his staff in his hand, chose five smooth stones from the stream, put them in the pouch of his shepherd's bag and, with his sling in his hand, approached the Philistine...As the Philistine moved closer to attack him, David ran quickly toward the battle line to meet him. Reaching into his bag and taking out a stone, he slung it and struck the Philistine on the forehead. The stone sank into his forehead, and he fell facedown on the ground. So David triumphed over the Philistine with a sling and a stone; without a sword in his hand he struck down the Philistine and killed him. (1 Sam. 17:32, 40, 48-50)

The Warrior King Conquers Jerusalem—2 Samuel 5: 6-10

The king and his men marched to Jerusalem to attack the Jebusites who lived there. The Jebusites said to David, "You will not get in here; even the blind and the lame can ward you off." They thought, "David cannot get in here. Nevertheless, David captured the fortress of Zion, the City of David. David then took up residence in the fortress and called it the City of David." (II Sam. 5:6-7)

The Ark Brought to Jerusalem—2 Samuel 6: 1-17

David again brought together out of Israel chosen men, thirty thousand in all. He and all his men set out from Baalah of Judah to bring up from there the ark of God, which is called by the Name, the Name of the Lord Almighty . . . . They brought the ark of the Lord and set it in its place inside the tent that David had pitched for it and David sacrificed burnt offerings and fellowship offerings before the Lord. (II Sam. 6:1-2, 17)

God's Promise to David, the Messianic Hope—2 Samuel 7: 6-16

The Lord declares to you that the Lord himself will establish a house for you: When your days are over and you rest with your fathers, I will raise up your offspring to succeed you, who will come from your own body, and I will establish his kingdom . . . . Your house and your kingdom will endure forever before me; your throne will be established forever. (II Sam 7:11b-12, 16)

THE CONTEXT

The story of David is found in 1 and 2 Samuel, 1 Kings, and 1 Chronicles. Like other stories we have reviewed, it is a composite of different writers and viewpoints. In some passages, David and Saul are portrayed in positive terms and negative in others. There are two different accounts of David's introduction to Saul and his court. In the first, David is recruited as a musician to soothe Saul's troubled mind (1 Samuel 16:14-23); in the second, he slays Goliath (1 Samuel 17:1-18-5).[78] There are also two different stories of the slaying of Goliath. In 1 Samuel 17:1-50 David, the young shepherd boy, triumphs over the giant; and in 2 Samuel 21:19, a certain Elhanan of Bethlehem is the victor. The Book of Chronicles omits David's flaws and foibles, whereas they are described in riveting detail in 1 and 2 Samuel and 1 Kings. These inconsistencies are noted to assist the reader in understanding the different viewpoints of events which are important for the context and interpretation of the texts.

The Books of 1 and 2 Samuel, initially a single scroll, probably had several literary sources.[79] The two books of Kings, also a single work before division, were edited by at least two different scribes.[80] Recent scholarship considers 1 and 2 Chronicles, originally a single book, to have been written in the fourth century BCE. Considered more sermon than narrative, Chronicles parallels the history of the books of Samuel and Kings. The author is highly selective in his choice of stories and material. In contrast to 1 and 2 Samuel and 1 Kings, he paints David in unblemished favorable light and focuses almost solely on events in the southern kingdom of Judah. Old Testament scholar Michael Wilcock concludes, "even the wickedness of the Davidic kings in the south are tidied out of the way."[81] The Chronicler, as he is often called, overwhelmingly favors the southern Judean viewpoint with Jerusalem as the capital, the Temple as the center of worship, and David as the Messianic hope.

These narratives emerged over centuries against a backdrop of political struggle and conquest. The monarchy began with Saul of Israel in the north, who was succeeded by David of Judah in the south. Following the death of David's successor, Solomon, the kingdom formally split: Israel in the north and Judah in the south. Both kingdoms fought against the Assyrians. Israel was conquered in 722 BCE and Assyria held Judah as a vassal kingdom. Later, when Judah rebelled, the Assyrians laid siege to Jerusalem in 701 BCE then mysteriously left. Babylon, a rising power, overthrew Judah in 586 BCE, beginning the Jewish Exile. Those are the broad historical strokes.

Against this grander scheme, Israel and Judah were struggling with each other for political and religious dominance of the Palestinian highlands, from Dan in the north to Beersheba in the south. Stories abounded about Saul, David, Solomon and their respective successors, down to Josiah of Judah, the last monarch in the Davidic line. These stories reflected the rivalry between Israel in the north and Judah in the south. Bethel was the northern religious center, Jerusalem was the southern. The storytellers and writers of the north put a positive spin on their kings and heroes and a biased negative description of those in the south. The story tellers and writers of the south responded in kind. Both were jockeying for eventual preeminence, and over time a propaganda campaign ensued for leverage and power in politics and religion. This snapshot history of the manuscripts which comprise the books of Samuel, Kings and Chronicles is an oversimplification, but sufficient for our purposes as they relate to the story of David and his rise from shepherd to messianic prototype and hope.

Narrative Overview

Saul was the first King of Israel, the Northern Kingdom; David was anointed the first king of Judah, the Southern Kingdom. David was eventually anointed king of the united kingdoms of Israel and Judah. David's reign lasted for 38 (or 39) years, 1000-962 BCE. He is the most legendary of all the kings of the Old Testament and occupies an exalted place in the history of the Jewish people. His popularity was still high at the time of the birth of Jesus, almost ten centuries after his death. His high ranking among the leaders of Israel is attested to by the fact that he is mentioned "nearly 800 times in the O.T., ca. sixty times in the N.T." [82]

When David appears on the scene, Saul has been anointed king by Samuel, the Philistines are in control of much of the high country, and they have captured the Ark. David gained sudden fame in his exploit of killing the giant Goliath (1Samuel 17:1-18:5)[83] David wins the hand of Michael, Saul's daughter. (1 Samuel 18:20, 27) As his name rises in fame and adulation, Saul's plummets in popularity.

In fits of psychological distress, Saul attempts to kill David. David, forced to flee for his life, becomes an outlaw living in the wilderness of Judah with his kinsmen, a group of desperados and malcontents. With this motley group of several hundred men, David joins the services of the Philistines where he is received with adulation and all the privileges of a vassal, including the gift of a town (Ziklag).

Following David's defection, Saul's army is soundly defeated by the Philistines at Mt. Gilboa. Saul fell on his own sword. His three sons were killed, including Jonathan, David's dear friend. The Philistines were entrenched in the central mountain plateau.

Earlier, David had been secretly anointed by Samuel to succeed Saul as King. At Hebron, following Saul's death, David's anointing is made official, and he is crowned king of Judah. (2 Samuel 2:1-4). He takes the throne of Judah while he is still the vassal of a foreign power, the Philistines. His power was consolidated when Saul's son, Eshbaal, a pretender to the throne was killed by two of David's own men. David is now anointed over Israel and the two kingdoms are united for the first time.

Next, David captures Jerusalem from the Jebusites and secures the capital. To consolidate religious power, he brings the Ark of the Covenant to Jerusalem and receives God's covenantal promise which establishes the messianic hope for eternity. Following those two significant events there are battles with enemies, palace intrigue, and family politics (the story of Bathsheba, Ammon and Tamar, Absalom). Before he dies, David has one final objective: a temple for the ark. Following the vision of an angel on the threshold of the Jebusite Araunah, David purchases the land for the temple. Though his son, Solomon, would build the temple, the foundation was laid for the home of the Priesthood and the Law, for the home of Judaism. What Moses had begun, David finished. All of the pieces in place— Jerusalem, Monarchy, Ark, Covenant, foundation for the Temple— David is ready to pass the crown to Solomon and begin the messianic dynasty.

Each of these elements of the story of David carried over into the early church and Christian message. They are indispensable in understanding the rise of Christianity. Learning objectives include exploring these key aspects of the story of David, how they developed, how they shaped western religions and politics, and their relevance for the 21st century. The legend of David and Goliath is the centerpiece of the saga, but his anointment by Samuel and consolidation of power are important aspects of the messianic legend.

The Anointment of David—1 Samuel 16:1-15

Three stories in 1 Samuel tell of David's emergence from obscurity to prominence: in the court of Saul, as a harpist (16:14-23), slaying Goliath (17:1-50), and his anointment by Samuel to be king (16:1-13).

All three seem to reflect an awareness of David's potential sacred greatness. But only one, the anointment by Samuel, has any semblance of a *call* in the tradition of Abraham and Moses.

When we first meet David, he is a shepherd boy, the youngest son of Jesse, and about to be anointed king of Judah by Samuel (16: 12), the last judge of Israel and greatest spiritual leader of Israel since Moses. Like Abraham and Moses before him, Samuel also receives a "call" from God (1 Samuel 3:1-18) and scripture suggests that through him God calls David.

At the house of Jesse of Bethlehem where God directed him, Samuel passes on Jesse's other sons. When David approaches, "ruddy, with a fine appearance and handsome features," the Lord says to Samuel, "Rise and anoint him; he is the one." (16:12b) The description of what happened next could be interpreted as the beginning of Christianity: "So Samuel took the horn or oil and anointed him in the presence of his brothers, and *from that day on the Spirit of the Lord came upon David in power.*" (16:13, italics added) The Messianic seed was sown. (The Hebrew word for "anointed one" is *mashiach* or "messiah." In Greek *mashiach* is translated *Christos* or Christ.)

Shepherd Warrior and Goliath—17:1-58

Following David's royal anointment by Samuel, he is summonsed by Saul to sooth the king with harp music (1 Samuel 16:14-23). He is described by one of Saul's servant's as **"a son of Jesse of Bethlehem who knows how to play the harp. He is a brave man and a warrior. He speaks well and is a fine-looking man. And the Lord is with him"** (I Sam. 16:17-18). Next, he enters the camp of the Israelites who are assembled in battle across the Valley of Elah from the Philistines. Goliath and his armament are described in great detail (17:4-7) and more background is provided on David's family. David had left his flock to take provisions to his brothers who were in the service of Saul. He arrives as each side is taking up battle positions, as they had done for forty days, to taunt each other.

The story of David and Goliath reminds us of other ancient epic gladiatorial duels (Hector and Ajax, Paris and Menelaus in *The Illiad.*) A champion is challenged and accepts the challenge. On-lookers are horrified. The armor of the duelists is described. Following speeches by the combatants, the fight begins. In the duel between David and Goliath, the weaker, less armed hero wins. The result was David's rise from the sheepfold, to shrewd politician, to national prominence.

This portrait of David, which contains his frailties and, at times, near scandalous behavior, is omitted by the Chronicler who begins with David's election as king over all of Israel (1 Chronicles 11:1) Though some question has been raised by historians regarding the Goliath event, historian John Bright convincingly states, "David's fame certainly rested on some spectacular feat, or feats, of this sort"[84]

The Warrior King Conquers Jerusalem—2 Samuel 5:1-10

Following the slaying of Goliath, Saul's royal position deteriorates and David's popularity climbs. With Saul's defeat at Gilboa and subsequent suicide, David is anointed at Hebron and crowned king over Judah and Israel where the Lord says to him, **"You shall shepherd my people Israel and you will become their ruler...and he reigned forty years"**(1 Samuel 5:1-4). "It is the classic tale of the rise of the young hero, a warrior of the true faith and a man of extraordinary charisma, who assumes the mantle of a failed leader and becomes the embodiment of his people's hopes and dreams."[85] According to scripture, he immediately marches on Jerusalem **to attack the Jebusites, who lived there.** (2 Samuel 5:6)

The manner in which the city was overthrown has always been of interest to historians and archaeologists. It is described in scripture as heavily guarded and presumed to be impregnable. David, with his personal troops and not those belonging to any of the tribes (2 Samuel 5:6), entered secretly through a water shaft and overthrew the defenders.[86]

In an attempt to raise his throne above tribal rights and distrusts and to unite the loyalties of the two kingdoms, David chooses a capital on a neutral site that is neither in the north or the south. (Our American forefathers—Alexander Hamilton, Thomas Jefferson, and James Madison—accomplished the same feat with the selection of Washington, D.C.) His next move is to defeat the Philistines. He inquires of the Lord:

> "Shall I go and attack the Philistines? Will you
>
> hand them over to me?"
>
> The Lord answered him, "Go, for I will surely
>
> hand the Philistines over to you."
>
> —2 Samuel 5;19

And scripture states, **David did as the Lord commanded him and he struck down the Philistines all the way from Gibeon to Gezer.** (2 Samuel 5:25) At this point, David is free of outside political danger and he focuses on consolidating his power.

David Brings the Ark of the Covenant to Jerusalem
—2 Samuel 6:1-17

David's second decision toward uniting his people was bringing the Ark of the Covenant to Jerusalem. His goal was to make Jerusalem the religious, as well as the political, capital of the young nation. He knew he needed to establish his throne on the foundations of the Mosaic tradition. "Through the Ark he sought to link the newly created state to Israel's ancient order as its legitimate successor, and to advertise the state as the patron and protector of the sacred institutions of the past."[87]

Arks were portable shrines and are known to have been used in the Near East, particularly in Egypt, Mesopotamia, and Canaan. The Israelite Ark of the Covenant is mentioned throughout the Old Testament. (Deuteronomy 10:2,5; Numbers 10:33; Joshua 6; 1 Samuel 4:2-8, 6:19, 7:1, 14:18; 2 Samuel 6:6-7, 17; 1 Kings 8:4-9, 12-13; 2 Kings 19:15; Jeremiah 3:15) In Exodus God gives Moses specific instructions regarding the design and construction of the Ark: . . . **have the people "make a chest of acacia wood—two and a half cubits long, a cubit and a half wide and a cubit and a half tall.** (25:10) It was to be overlaid with "pure gold" inside and out and edged with gold molding. Additional details included the design of the poles and rings to carry the Ark, a gold "atonement cover" and cherubim bracketing the cover. The Testimony, or Law, given to Moses on Sinai was to be placed in the Ark. (Exodus 25:11-22)[88] The Ark, along with the Tabernacle, was an indispensable part of the Hebrews journey in the Wilderness. Early on the Ark was a direct manifestation of God's presence and was identified with him. In Numbers 10:35-36, Moses actually addresses the Ark as God. The Philistines considered the Ark equivalent to God. 1(Samuel 4:6-8).

For a long time the Ark resided at Shiloh, a central sanctuary in the times of the tribal confederacy. In 1 Samuel, the Ark is captured by the Philistines at Ebenezer (4:1-11), causes deadly havoc among the Philistine people, and triumphantly returns to Israel. During Philistine occupation, it was concealed at Kirjath-jearim where it had been neglected for a generation since the fall of the sanctuary of Shiloh. David's transferal of the Ark to Jerusalem was a difficult feat. The story of Uzzah falling dead upon touching the Ark to steady it is a familiar one. Perhaps less familiar is the scene where David's wife Michael, daughter of Saul, confronts and scolds him for dancing naked in the streets **"in the sight of the slave girls of his servants as any vulgar fellow would"**(2 Samuel 6:20).

When the Ark was situated under a tent in Jerusalem, the city became Zion, the City of God. God's presence was once again "tabernacled" among his people. By placing the Ark of the Covenant beneath the "Tent of Meeting," (2 Samuel 7:2) David was linking two sacred objects from the Mosaic era.[89] Stationing the Ark in Jerusalem shifted the religious center of Israel from Shiloh and "the event was probably reenacted annually with Psalm 132 as the liturgy of the festival."[90] A monarchy, as well as a royal theology, was beginning to emerge.

God's Promise to David, The Messianic Hope—2 Samuel 7:1-16

When King David is comfortably **settled in his palace** (2 Samuel 7:1) he receives from God through the prophecy of Nathan, the assurance and pledge of his throne from God. Ironically, David's plan included building a temple for the Ark (**"Here I am living in a palace of cedar, while the ark of the Lord remains in a tent"**—7:20) Nathan initially supports David's plan (7:3) but rejects it after hearing from God. The following passage resonates throughout Jewish history and theology:

I have not dwelt in a house from the day I brought the Israelites up out of Egypt to this day. I have been moving from place to place with a tent as my dwelling... I took you from the pasture and from following the flock to be ruler over my people Israel...Now I will make your name great, like the names of the greatest men of the earth. And I will provide a place for my people Israel and will plant them so that they can have a home of their own and no longer be disturbed...The Lord declares to you that the Lord himself will establish a house for you...Your house and your kingdom will endure forever before me; your throne will be established forever

—2 Samuel 7:8-16

With the ark as the center of this background, the Lord makes his covenant with David and his throne for eternity. Ark and Covenant become inseparable in the mindset of the people of Israel. David had rescued and returned the Ark of God's Covenant, the receptacle of God's promises to his people to the new national capital. The great heroes of the faith before David—Noah, Abraham, and Moses—had covenants with the Lord. Because of David's efforts, Israel occupied the land, and that possession of sacred territory was a testament to Abraham's enduring covenant. It seemed only proper the covenant should be renewed for David's lineage under his reign. Psalm 132 reiterates this oath of Yahweh: "The Lord swore an oath to David, a sure oath that he will not revoke . . . . For the Lord has chosen Zion . . . . This is my resting place forever and ever...I will make a horn grow for David and set up a lamp for my anointed one" (vv 11, 13-14, 17; Lamentations 3:22 also echoes the Davidic Covenant.) In essence, the wearer of the crown becomes a son of God. This theme would emerge again in the New Testament with Jesus Christ, the Messiah or anointed one.

Nathan performs the prophet's task and conveys the message. David responds in worship and prays, "that all that the Lord has spoken may be fulfilled and that through it all the greatness of the Lord may become obvious to all."[91] Then, like many heroes whose flaws become their downfall, David's life begins to unravel.

The Bathsheba Affair—2 Samuel 11:1-12:25

The story of David and Bathsheba has been over-dramatized and glamorized by Hollywood. The tale contributes little to the key elements of the David epic—Jerusalem, Temple, Ark, Covenant, Messiah—that would figure prominently in later Judaism and in the New Testament. The element of infidelity and lust is a key religious theme, and the next king in the Davidic line, Solomon, was a result of David's relationship with Bathsheba.

The focus of the story is on an encounter David has with the prophet Nathan. (2 Samuel 12) The Bathsheba affair is background. David is king. He has vanquished the Philistines, conquered Jerusalem and secured it as the capital city, moved the Ark of the Covenant to Jerusalem, and solidified his power base over the tribal confederacy. The Covenant has been renewed and David's throne has been established for perpetuity. The Lord will never stop loving him. What more could a man want?

From the roof of his palace one evening David observes Bathsheba bathing. **The woman was very beautiful** (11:2b), and he desires her. He inquires and learns she was the wife of Uriah, one of the king's faithful warriors. Lustful stories move quickly and scripture states, **She came to him and he slept with her** (11:4) Bathsheba becomes pregnant. David brings Uriah home from battle to sleep with his wife. Uriah is a disciplined warrior and refuses to sleep with his wife while he is serving on active duty. (11:11) In a second attempt to manipulate Uriah, David seeks to weaken his will by causing him to become drunk. The attempt fails. David's remaining option, to murder Uriah, is accomplished by having Uriah intentionally placed in the front line of battle.

This act would seem the "perfect murder." But, the prophet Nathan was aware of the plot. What follows is one of the most dramatic confrontations in The Bible. (2 Samuel 12:1-14) Hollywood portrays Nathan striding boldly into the royal throne room, planting his staff with each step with the audience parting for him as he approaches David on his throne. Scripture does not reveal to us where the encounter took place or who was present but sets the scene without embellishment: **The Lord sent Nathan to David. When he came to him he said, "There were two men in a certain town . . . . "** (12:1) David naively listens to the parable of another man whose behavior parallels his own, and scripture says he **burned with anger against the man and said to Nathan, "As surely as the Lord lives, the man who did this deserves to die . . . . Then Nathan said to David, "You are the man!"** (12:7). Nathan does not relax his point but drives it home. He lists all the Lord has given to David, but because David dared to **"despise the word of the Lord by doing what is evil in his sight,"** Nathan admonishes him: **" . . . the sword will never depart from your house...Out of your own household I am going to bring calamity upon you"**(12: 9-11).

David's response to this stern lecture of doom and gloom suggests remorse and penitence, but scripture reports only his words, **I have sinned against the Lord.** (12:13) He does not ask forgiveness, yet Nathan tells him, **The Lord has taken away your sin.** (12:13) The son Bathsheba has borne, however, will die, Nathan says. David fasts. He lies prostrate on the ground for days pleading for the child. After seven days the child dies and David **washed, put on lotion and changed his clothes...went into the house of the Lord and worshiped.** (12:20) He then goes to his own house and eats in a casual manner that raises the brow of his staff. When they inquire about his sudden change in mood, he responds, **"But now that he is dead, why should I fast? Can I bring him back again? I will go to him but he will not return to me."** (12:23) The narrative next says David has sex with Bathsheba and Solomon was born.

David has been forgiven. He has another son, Solomon. All seems well. Yet in the remainder of the "Court History" the reader can easily discern how this one incident, like a cancer, corrupts his house and spreads, wave upon wave, through his entire family. Amnon forces sex with his virgin half-sister, Tamar. In revenge, Absalom kills Amnon. Absalom, alienated from his father, foments a rebellion and is murdered by Joab. One of the most vivid of Old Testament scriptures, one that inspired William Faulkner's great novel *Absalom, Absalom*, portrays David's anguish upon hearing the sad news:

And the king was deeply moved, and went up to

The chamber over the gate, and wept; and as he

Went, he said, "O my son Absalom, my son, my son

Absalom! Would I had died instead of you, O

Absalom, my son, my son.

—2 Samuel 18:33

Nathan's prophesy—**Out of your own household I am going to bring calamity upon you**—came true. Following Solomon, the product of the fateful marriage, the united kingdom of Israel split never to be reunited.

THE MESSAGE

The Anointment of David—1 Samuel 16:1-15

David, the eighth son of Jesse, is the youngest and the least likely for royal anointment and to become Israel's hope. Abraham was seventy-five years of age when he was called by God. We do not know the age of Moses when he experienced his call at the burning bush, but scripture suggests he was probably middle-aged. He had married the young Midianite woman (Exodus 2:21) and was tending the flock of his father-in-law.

Several decades ago there was much discussion about the "generation gap" with the general theme that youth could not be trusted. Many of the leaders of the Old Testament were approximately the youthful age of the founders of our country. Thomas Jefferson was thirty-two years old when he wrote the Declaration of Independence.

George Washington became Commander-in-Chief of the Continental Army at age forty-three. Alexander Hamilton became an artillery captain under Washington at age twenty and the first Secretary of Treasury before he was thirty. At age thirty-five Martin Luther King, Jr. became the youngest person to receive the Nobel Peace Prize for his civil rights leadership and accomplishments. Alexander the Great conquered the known world when he was thirty-three years old. Joan of Arc led a French army at age nineteen. Putting these examples in perspective, the youthfulness of David made him a probable choice to unite Israel and Judea, establish a monarchic dynasty, and become a messianic proto-type. He was no more an improbable candidate to accomplish those objectives than Jesus of Nazareth was to assume that same messianic role and launch the Christian faith at age thirty.

When Samuel anointed David, the young shepherd became the "anointed one," the *mashiach,* or the messiah. The three terms are interchangeable. The event would become significant centuries later, probably during the reign of Josiah, the last great monarch of the Davidic line. In the 21st century, the anointing of David is viewed as the beginning of a royal dynastic process that morphed into a messianic theology. The Jewish monarchy vanished in the sixth century BCE and was replaced by the Temple and its cadre of priests. Upon its destruction, the Temple was replaced by a messianic hope. At some point in the future, the "anointed one," or messiah, would return. For early Christianity, which was initially a Jewish reform movement, that messiah was Jesus of Nazareth, the *Christ*, which is Greek for "anointed one." For Christians today, the Christ embodies a theology of hope. He is the expectant Messiah of the future, but also comes daily in our lives.

David's role as shepherd is significant. The most prominent leaders of the Old Testament—Abraham and Moses—were shepherds, a symbolic theme that appeared in the New Testament with Jesus of Nazareth. He used the metaphor frequently, and in the Gospel of John, he referred to himself as the good shepherd (10:11). The writer of 1 Peter refers to his audience as "the shepherds of God's flock" (5:2) and to Jesus as "the Chief Shepherd" (5: 4) Caring for and serving others is a powerful and distinguished symbol of fulfilling our roles as shepherds that stretches back through the millennia to the beginnings of the Judeo-Christian tradition.

Another motif in this story is God's ability to look past appearances and the heart of the person. Often we confuse reality with appearance. Today's society is encouraged to use products that promote looking good, looking younger or feeling better. We ignore the realities and go for the appearance.

God finds grace in the least likely sources and places as revealed by review of David's family tree. His grandmother was an immigrant Moabite woman, and the lineage of his grandfather, Boaz, included a Canaanite adulteress, Tamar (Genesis 20), and a Canaanite prostitute, Rehab (Joshua 2). Nothing in David's ancestral history suggested royalty. But God's plans often operate on a different principle: "The last shall be first . . . . " (Matthew 19:30, 20:16; Mark 10:31; Luke 13:30). Jesus was born in a stable. His father was a carpenter. He was crucified as a felon. Yet, Jesus became the Anointed One, the Messiah. According to the Gospel of Matthew, his ancestral lineage included the names of Tamar, Rehab, Ruth . . . and David.

The Shepherd Warrior and Goliath—1 Samuel 17:1-58

David's triumph over Goliath has become a metaphor for underdogs who hope to win contests. "This story has been told and retold, especially by the weak, the oppressed, the marginal, and the powerless—those who do not simply hope for a David but see themselves as David, faced with the giants of oppression, and who know that their only hope lies with a living God."[92] Because of the drama and imagery, this type of story has a natural appeal for all ages. Perhaps Paul was referring to this story when he wrote in 1 Corinthians that "God chose the foolish things of the world to shame the wise; God chose the weak things of the world to shame the strong" (1:27).

Though it relates to the underdog theme, the key message of the story is basically about faith, not one's size or weapons. In the story, David does possess courage. He also knows how to use a slingshot with deadly accuracy. But David, the shepherd, knows of other resources. His win signals the beginning of his job. He will face tough battles that are more deadly than Goliath or human giants. David knows he must have faith in the Lord and trust in His strength, guidance, and truth. His faith emerges in his two speeches associated with this event. He affirms the higher spirit of the Lord and says, "All those gathered here will know that it is not by sword or spear that the Lord saves; for the battle is the Lord's..." (1 Samuel 17:47). The story of David and Goliath takes place within a larger story of David's faith and Saul's lack of faith and the one who, in the long run, endures. These themes are as relevant today as they were in biblical times.

The Warrior King Conquers Jerusalem—2 Samuel 5:1-10

These few verses are packed with several significant concepts. The king will be a shepherd and caretaker, not a tyrant. He will covenant with his people and not hoard power. Throughout the Bible the shepherd image dominates: "The Lord is my shepherd" (Psalm 23:1) and the good shepherd "lays down his life for the sheep" (John 10:11). David did not always exemplify the role of sacrificial shepherd, but the scriptures uphold the image. "This brief passage only lifts these images briefly into view, but it is a beginning in David that points us to rich new understandings of God's kingdom for Israel's future and for our own."[93]

The newness of Israel's kingdom begins with David and Jerusalem. As noted in the exegesis, Jerusalem at this point had no connection with Israel but was affiliated with a Canaanite tribe, the Jebusites. The future of Israel bonds inseparably with David and Jerusalem. Jerusalem becomes the City of David. Centuries later when the city is conquered and the Temple is destroyed, Jerusalem becomes "the Jerusalem that is above is free, and she is our mother. (Galatians 4:26. *The King James Version* reads "But Jerusalem which is above is free, which is the mother of us all."

The Jerusalem of the 21st century is not free. Today, it is a divided between Jews, Christians, and Muslims. The holy Christian sites are further divided among varying denominations that jealously guard their small dominions. Jerusalem has become a city of walls and barriers. The hope for the eradication of these walls and the advent of peace lies in the scripture, "she is our mother." When the three major religions of the world that claim Jerusalem as a religious center realize the hope of their heritage and tradition then the city can fulfill its name and become a symbol of peace. When they realize this city is God's place, not their own private real estate, God's presence will again radiate.

David Brings the Ark of the Covenant to Jerusalem
—2 Samuel 6:1-17

Moving the Ark of the Covenant to Jerusalem would be analogous today to moving the Plymouth Rock to Washington D.C. That comparison may be an overstatement but David's act of moving the Ark of the Covenant was tantamount to eclipsing the national shine at Shiloh where it had resided for generations. Moving the Ark of the Covenant meant changing the old order and old religion and making way for the new. Moving the Ark of the Covenant to Jerusalem laid the foundation for the mega-church of that era. There were those who were against the new order, against moving a venerated shine to the city. There were those who wanted the same old religion in the same old venerated places.

Are there shrines that need to be moved today? Many rural churches in America are vanishing. Churches with names like Shiloh, Ebenezer and Bethel could be saved through consolidation, but congregations refuse to leave the cemeteries attached to the church grounds. Should movement be in the other direction, should mega-churches be reducing their size and dispersing? Are there shrines that should be abolished? Walls come to mind, in particular the walls in current Palestine, the Mexican border wall. Should some "arks," or shrines, be rehabilitated? The commercialization of venerated sites in the Holy Land diminishes their sacred meaning. Are there shrines that should not be built? Some orthodox Jews want to build a third Temple on the Temple Mount encroaching on Muslim shrines, a move that would exacerbate an already tenuous situation.

From another perspective, the Ark of the Covenant symbolized the presence of God, as though all of the deity was funneled into one small box. On a larger scale, do we attach a similar meaning to our churches and sanctuaries? This is the place where God abides. We must go there to feel his presence. How would Jesus have felt about the Ark of the Covenant? He came to fulfill the Covenant and in some ways is identified with the New Covenant. Holy Communion is a celebration of the New Covenant: "This is my blood of the covenant which is poured out for many . . . ." (Matthew 26:28; Mark 14:24). Jesus realized the danger of this type of thinking and encouraged people to worship God in spirit, not in the confines of a particular place. In today's parlance, Jesus was going "outside the box." At his crucifixion the Temple veil was rent unleashing God's spirit from its sacred enclosure into the secular world.

God's Promise to David, The Messianic Hope—2 Samuel 7:6-16

This chapter has been called one of the most important in the entire Bible. The consequences of this oath are enormous and would become apparent in later times when it would be renewed and reinterpreted for the times at hand. The prophetic covenant is "the historical origin and legitimation of all messianic expectations."[94] The Messianic proto-type and model of behavior was set for those who would regain control of the Temple.

During the rule of the Hasmoneans, sectarian groups splintered apart from mainstream Judaism. Messianic visions and messianic leaders repeatedly rose up to challenge the Romans but also "to set models of righteous behavior to be followed in order to regain control of the Temple from a wicked, illegitimate priesthood and to lead the people of Israel piously."[95] All of these historical consequences revert to this one passage of scripture.

This passage of scripture also suggests a close relationship between theology and political ideology. God risks by engaging his agenda in the political arena. Are we not called to do the same? Did not Jesus call his disciples to "go into all the world," which means the world of politics? We live in a democracy, not a theocracy which was the model of government for Israel in the Old Testament, and in some ways continues in Israel today. Israel claims to be a democracy, yet much of their secular law is rooted in religious law. These are difficult passages for a democracy where church and state are separated so that democracy might survive. Nevertheless, the text does call us to inject our faith and Christian values into the political arena. We must work publicly for a better state, country, and world. This theme is continuous from Genesis through Revelation.

This passage is about God's unconditional grace and his judgment. God's promise, however, does not remove the subjunctive "if." Kings will be chastised if they go astray. The indicative of God's grace in his promise also includes the imperative of our moral action and behavior. Sin has its consequences. We are forgiven but are instructed to, "go and sin no more," as Jesus told the adulteress. (John 8:11)

God's enduring promise and hope in this passage may be one of the reasons Israel has survived. King Louis IV once asked Voltaire to give him proof for the existence of God. Voltaire is said to have replied, "The Jews, my Lord, the Jews." And the Jews hang their religious and national hopes on this scripture, this warranty that their house will endure forever.

The spirit of this promise passed into Christian hands in the early first century. Most of those Christians were Jews looking for reform within their own religion. They found hope in this passage of a new messiah. They saw Jesus as the bearer of this renewed promise. Because he was born in the line of David, he inherited the same promise and hope. This was bedrock for these early Christians. Jesus announced a New Kingdom with a different unlimited transforming power. The entire Incarnation concept is based upon God's promise through Nathan to David. If we are to know God's promises, we must risk involvement in his world; the "word" must "become flesh." This promise made long ago, must be renewed daily. Incarnation means being involved with the Messiah. We must renew daily, in very concrete and substantive ways, the hope of God's promise to others, "for one of the least of these brothers of mine" (Matthew 25:40)

The Bathsheba Affair—2 Samuel 11:1-12:25

Taken at face value, there is nothing amazing about the plot of this story. We have heard it before. It reminds us of today's headlines, and men and women with power, stretching back through political history who seemingly "have it all," yet desire more. We are reminded of Henry Kissinger's famous quotation, that "Power is the ultimate aphrodisiac."[96] What is amazing about the story is that it is even in the Bible and that it is told of David, the messianic prototype. Yet, there it is, stark and real and haunting. "It is a testimony to the realism of the Israelite faith that a tragedy like this could be written. Because the David story ascends the heights of human aspiration and plumbs the depths of human anguish it has outlived the practical circumstances from which it came. In one sense David was a victim of his own greatness, of an indomitable will that urged him to scale the tempting heights of power . . . ."[97]

The lessons of the story relate to any century. A small, seemingly insignificant sin of desire can lead to monstrous behavior, to murder. "You shall not covet," (Exodus 20:17) says the tenth commandment. Do not even consider the thought because it can lead to the deed, which in turn leads to other deeds which kill and destroy and leave you empty-handed. The writer of the Book of James in the New Testament confirms: "You want something but don't get it. You kill and covet but you cannot have what you want." (4:2) One wonders why the last commandment was not placed further up the ranking order, at least before the seventh commandment, "you shall not commit adultery" (Exodus 20:14); or the sixth, "you shall not murder" (Exodus 20:13). Jesus demonstrated his understanding of human nature when he equated the thought with the deed.

This incident that began as a thought while walking on his roof corrupted David's entire house. But "I like," became "I want." After that came the incest of Amnon and Tamar, the revolt of Absalom and his murder. We might reflect on our own homes and domestic situations, the sins we commit that affect our family members, neighbors, and society. Many people are hurt because a wayward thought took the next step. In the United States, the sin of slavery exemplifies how one sin polluted and corrupted a nation. Sins, though they can be forgiven, are once and for all. They infect entire systems, pervade, and harm its relationships.

One of the most human elements of this story is reflected in David's pharisaic, holier-than-thou reaction. It is easy to condemn the scandals of others: "You, hypocrite, first take the plank out of your own eye, and then you will see clearly to remove the speck from your brother's eye" (Matthew 7:5) Prior to that statement Jesus said, "Do not judge or you will be judged" (Matthew 7:1) Paul wrote to the Corinthians "So, if you think you are standing firm, be careful that you don't fall" (1 Corinthians 10:12). Does David attempt to rid himself of his guilty conscience by passing judgment on someone else? Eventually, Nathan gets through to him and he realizes that he was the man, the one who sinned. At that point David was remorseful. Psalm 32 is acknowledged as David's expression on the event—"Blessed is he whose transgressions are forgiven, whose sins are covered; Blessed is the man whose sin the Lord does not count against him." (vv. 1-2) Psalm 51 also expresses David's contrition: "Have mercy on me, O God, according to your unfailing love; according to your great compassion blot out my transgressions. Wash away all my iniquity and cleanse me from all sin" (vv. 1-2) Gerhard Anderson points out that, "In a deeper sense David was involved in the conflict with the God he sought to serve, the God with whose will he had to reckon in the practical affairs of daily life."[98]

Often interpretations of the story omits Bathsheba's point of view. She was the victim of David's lust and must have suffered greatly. She lost her reputation, gave birth to an illegitimate child, lost a husband, married her lover, and lost a child. Some have said she participated in the sin. Is this a rationalization? David was King. Teachers, counselors, pastors are figures of authority and figures of authority who can abuse their powerful role by manipulating the weakness of others, a problem that has greatly affected the Catholic Church and other denominations. The Elmer Gantrys have been revealed.

In the long run David benefits. He was guilty but forgiven and taken back into the loving relationship with God; the woman he desired became his wife; their son became the next king. Many Christians today find this form of forgiveness, this success after the fact, unacceptable. Society is not often forgiving and people who have committed sins find difficulty in forgiving themselves. The mission of the church is to reclaim sinners, which includes all people. The church's faithfulness in that mission fulfills its commission by the risen Christ. (Matthew 28:18-20; Mark 16:15; Luke 24:46-47; Acts 1:8; John 21:15-19) The forgiven are also called to repent, turn around, don't do it again. David did not repent. Do we repent when we are forgiven?

David was forgiven, but he also paid the price for his sin. God's hand of mercy is equally balanced with his hand of judgment. We have a moral imperative to respond appropriately to God's free grace. Jesus said to the adulteress brought to him, "Go now and leave your life of sin" (John 8:11) To the invalid at the Pool of Bethesda, he said, "Stop sinning or something worse may happen to you" John 5:14.

QUESTIONS FOR FURTHER STUDY AND DISCUSSION

1. What does the concept of Messiah mean for us today?
2. What are our counterparts today of the "Ark of the Covenant?" What sacred shrines need to be moved, cleansed, and abolished? What changes are occurring today that are similar to the change David made in moving the Ark of the Covenant to the capital city?
3. What additional examples can you give in which the sins of fathers and mothers infected an entire family or country?
4. Did God's granting restoration of fellowship to David encourage wrongdoing? Is this an example of positive reinforcement of sin?
5. Where can you identify places, times in your life when you were forgiven and you did not repent. What were the consequences? Identify times in your life when you were forgiven and you repented, you left that way of life. What were those consequences?

Chapter Nine

Esther

THE TEXT

> Then Esther sent this reply to Mordecai: "Go, gather
> together all the Jews who are in Susa, and fast for me. Do
> not eat or drink for three days, night or day. I and my maids
> will fast as you do. When this is done, I will go to the king,
> even though it is against the law. And if I perish, I perish. (
>
> —Genesis 4:15-16

THE CONTEXT

The Book of Esther, the seventeenth book of the Christian Old
Testament, is positioned between Nehemiah and Job. In some ancient
manuscripts it follows the Pentateuch. Authorship is unknown, but
Esther was probably written in Persia. The background and action of
the story occur in the eastern Jewish Diaspora of the Persian Empire
during the 5th century or later, and the plot unfolds in the court at Susa,
one of the four Persian capitals. The author provides significant details
about the Persian court setting and customs. Jews were widely
dispersed throughout the Persian empire through the fifth and fourth
centuries BCE. Over time they had adjusted to Persian rule and were
dependent economically upon the empire.

Most scholars date Esther around the late fourth or early third
century, no earlier than the reign of the Emperor Xerxes (486-465
BCE) who is Ahasuerus in the story.[99] *The Interpreter's Dictionary of
the Bible* considers a date of composition, "in the late Persian or Greek
period, and probably the latter. The language suggest the Hellenistic
period."[100]

141

Esther differs from most Old Testament books because it is *written* literature. This means there is no indication of an oral tradition. During Purim, the scroll of the book was supposed to be read and the book may have been written for this purpose.[101]

Esther is a short story or novella comparable to Ruth and has also been compared to Daniel and the court stories of Joseph (Genesis 37-50)[102] It is the final book of the five scrolls, "a tale of Jewish courage amid the threats and risks of the Persian empire."[103] Some scholars have classified Esther as a "historical novella" but there is no historical evidence of any of the key characters.[104] Xerxes, identified as Ahasuerus, was a great king of an empire which extended from India to Ethiopia. Susa was one of the capitals of the empire. But there is no record of Esther, Mordecai, or Haman. Xerxes' queen was Amestris throughout his reign. There is no historical evidence of a massacre during his reign.[105] Esther is classified by some scholars as a festival legend for the Jewish Purim, a celebration for their deliverance from an ethnic cleansing similar to the extermination of the Jews ordered by Hitler.[106]

Esther has a unified simple short story structure (character→event→ change) and single plot with a clear beginning, middle, and end. The status and character of the main characters undergo change by the story's conclusion. The fast-paced action occurs within a specified time frame. "It contains all the elements of a popular romance novel: a young and beautiful heroine; a wicked, scheming villain; a wise old father figure; and an inept and laughable ruler."[107] Beneath the surface are darker themes of racial intolerance, threats of ethnic cleansing through genocide, and the recurring Old Testament themes of pride and vanity. In the end, good triumphs over evil reflecting an apocalyptic perspective similar to that found in the Book of Daniel. *The HarperCollins Bible Dictionary* points to three prominent aspects of the story: (1) God is not mentioned, (2) the protagonist is a woman, and (3) instructions from the Torah define Jewish life.[108]

The Book of Esther has drawn criticism by Jews and Christians. There is no mention of God in the book, no prayer, no religious activity or reference to the Temple. "The book of Esther itself, however, seems deliberately to avoid specific references to God or to religious practice."[109] Esther does order (4:16) a fast but its function is secular with no mention of God. Neither Esther nor Mordecai follow the Torah. Esther marries a Gentile and eats non-kosher food. She is so completely non-Jewish in her demeanor and behavior that she blends with the non-Jewish court. The book does consistently pursue one objective, an explanation for the celebration and observance of the traditional Jewish festival of Purim. "The omission of reference to God is understandable in a book intended to be read at a festival of merry-making, noise, and conviviality. The major theme of the book, persecution returning on the head of those who initiate it, leads through all the details of the story to the final victory which Purim celebrates."[110]

For some of the reasons cited above, *Esther* was contested within both Jewish and Christian canon. "The early Jewish comments on the text show their concern to make the religious aspect of the book more apparent."[111] Wesley J. Fuerst notes, "No Christian commentary was written on it for seven centuries, and it failed to appear in many lists of biblical books in the early church, especially in the eastern Mediterranean area."[112] Though most books of the Old Testament were discovered in the Dead Sea Scrolls, not a single fragment of Esther was among them.[113] Martin Luther denounced the book in the sixteenth century, stating it lacked theology.

Despite those concerns, the Book of Esther was immensely popular. During the Middle Ages numerous copies circulated. "It was 'The Scroll' above the other four, in Jewish references."[114] Jewish people, who underwent periodic persecution, identified with Mordecai, "The Jew" in the story. He endures because he is Jewish (6:13) and Jews saw his triumph as their triumph.

The Story

The Book of Esther opens with a feast orchestrated by Ahasuerus, king of Persia, who orders his wife Vashti to parade her beauty before the banquet guests. When she refuses, Ahasuerus removes her as queen and orders 1400 selected young women into his court. From the group the king picks Esther, a young orphan promoted by her cousin

Mordechai, to be the new queen. Esther conceals she is a Jew. Soon after her promotion, Mordechai learns of a plot to assassinate Ahasuerus and informs the king. The plot is aborted and Mordechai's service to the king is documented in the court records.

Ahasuerus appoints Haman as his prime minister. Mordechai refuses to bow to Haman. Haman, in his outrage, learns Mordichai is a Jew and implements plans to kill not only Mordechai, but all of the Jews in the empire. Ahasuerus grants permission for Haman to execute this plan. Lots are cast to choose the date which is the thirteenth of the month of Adar. Mordechai discovers the plans and orders widespread penitence and fasting. Esther follows suit requesting that all Jews fast and pray for three days with her. On the third day she has an audience with Ahasuerus and invites him to a feast in the presence of Haman. During the feast, Esther requests their attendance at another feast the following evening. Meanwhile, Haman is offended again by Mordechai and orders gallows erected for him.

During the evening Ahasuerus has insomnia and orders the court's records read to him to help him sleep. During the reading, the king learns of Mordechai's services in the earlier plot against his life and is told Mordechai has received no recognition for saving the king's life. Haman appears and King Ahasuerus asks the prime minister, "What should be done for the man the king delights to honor?" Haman, thinking the king wishes to honor him, suggests the man be attired in the king's royal robes and paraded on the king's royal horse. Haman is mortified when instructed to honor Mordechai in the fashion Haman recommended.

Later that evening, Ahasuerus and Haman attend Esther's second banquet. She reveals she is Jewish and reveals Haman's plans to exterminate her people, which includes her. Outraged, Ahasuerus exits the banquet room. Haman remains and pleads with Esther for his life. The king returns, perceives Haman is sexually assaulting the queen, and orders Haman hanged on the gallows erected for Mordecai. Ahasuerus cannot cancel the previous decree against the Jews, but he grants them permission to defend themselves during attacks. On 13 Adar, five hundred anti-Jewish assailants, including Haman's ten sons, are killed and tens of thousands in the empire are massacred by the

Jews. In the conclusion, Mordechai gains a prominent position in Ahasuerus' court and institutes an annual commemoration of the delivery of the Jewish people from extermination.

THE MESSAGE

Drawing theological perspectives on a literary production where the word God or references to God never appear is difficult and may seem impossible. Though they are not outwardly theological, Esther presents universal themes that carry profound theological messages. Some of the great truths of the Bible are not *prima facia,* they do not float on the surface of the words but emerge from greater depths. In other words, one must read "between the lines." Esther is one of those books, like Jonah, where the message may not be immediate but comes to the reader after several trips through its pages.

A good example of Esther's theological depth is paradoxically reflected in the absence of any reference to God. Deity is not mentioned. Was this an oversight on the part of the writer, or an intentional literary ploy designed to make a point? A correlate question might be, "Does one have to evoke God's name to witness his love?" Esther takes a courageous stand for her people and their faith. She has no need to mention her God. Her witness and testimony of faith are sufficient.

Nearly a century ago, a similar testimony of God's love occurred. A young woman, Elsa Brändström, became dissatisfied with a life of wealth and royalty. Her father, Edvard Brändström, became Swedish Ambassador at the court of the Russian Tsar Nicholas II. Elsa spent much of her early life watching the soldiers through palace windows as they marched off to war and decided to volunteer as a nurse in the Russian army. In 1915, she traveled to Siberia for the Swedish Red Cross to introduce basic medical treatment for the German prisoners of war. In St. Petersburg she founded a Swedish Aid Organization. During the Russian Revolution, she persisted and continued her work until she was arrested in 1920. Throughout her treatment of soldiers, on and off the battlefield, she was never known to utter the word "God." Yet she became known as the "Angel of Siberia" and became famous as the "patron saint of soldiers." Elsa Brändström was a latter-day Esther.

Esther's story would be incomplete without her cousin, Mordecai. Due to her parents' untimely death, Mordecai had helped raise Esther. (Esther 2:7) Mordecai's skills and wisdom as a politician were involved in the plan for King Xerses to notice Esther. Esther not only got the king's attention, he chose her as his queen.

Esther and Mordecai become heroes of their people. To honor their memory and recognize their saving act on behalf of their people, the observance of Purim is observed by faithful Jews all over the world. "The result of such practice is that every generation of Jews has the opportunity to engage again in the daring task of Jewish particularity in the public life of the world."[115] Like Moses before them, Esther and Mordecai led their people back from "death" to "life,' a smaller version of the Exodus from Egyptian slavery. Similar to Esther's courageous attitude, "If we perish, we perish."

In almost every generation and nation, the need arises for individuals to "stand" against potential atrocities waged against ethnic groups or races. In most of these cases, as in *Esther*, the "Hamans" have no proof for their charges. Two illustrations are historically prominent.

Though unsuccessful, many people stood against Hitler in his efforts to solve "the Jewish problem." If the United States and other enlightened European nations had intervened earlier, the Holocaust might have been avoided. There were those who tried to intercede on behalf of the Jews, but their efforts were too little and too late. Hitler had sowed the seeds of destruction and many had accepted his master plan. Many Christians acquiesced just to keep peace in Germany. Like Esther and Mordecai, some heroes took a different course. Elsa Brändström surfaced again, this time raising money for orphans in Germany. Dietrich Bonheoffer refused the offer from friends to settle in the U. S. and remained in Germany to assist the German Resistance Movement and help found the Confessing Church in opposition to the Nazi state church. He was martyred only hours before the Allied liberation.

Another example of persecution and murder occurred in the American South. Hangings, shootings and harassment of African-Americans were commonplace during the 19th and 20th centuries, reaching a climax during the struggle for civil rights in the latter half of the 20th century. Again, "good people" stood by and let the injustices continue. Following the examples of Esther and Mordica, a few took a stand: Fanny Lou Hammer and Rosa Parks; Martin Luther King, Jr., Medger Evers, and James Meredith. Like Esther, these brave souls refused to let parochial laws supersede a higher law of God's love and care for all humankind. They refused to let injustice run its course. If they perished, they perished. The world needs more Esthers and Mordicais to stand in the gap wherever injustice exists and threatens human rights.

Another powerful inspiration reflected in Esther is her profile in courage in the face of death. She knows she is literally putting her body on the line: **If I perish, I perish.** (4:16b) She accepts the ultimate consequence with calm dignity and brave resignation. A similar attitude is reflected in Jesus of Nazareth in his final hours: "My Father, if it is possible, may this cup be taken from me. Yet not as I will, but as you will. (See also Mark 14:36 and Luke 22:42). In his moment of death, Jesus says, "Father into your hands I commit my spirit" (Luke 23:46). Paul echoes a similar faith: "For if we live, we live to the Lord; and if we die, we die to the Lord. So, whether we live or die, we belong to the Lord" (Romans 14:8) In Philippians he states, "For me to live is Christ and to die is gain" (1:21).

Esther's statement, **If I perish, I perish**, also foreshadows Jesus of Nazareth's paradox of faith and freedom when he says, "Whosoever finds his life will lose it, and whoever loses his life for my sake will find it" (Matthew 10:39) The idea of finding one's life by losing it is mentioned by Jesus in all four New Testament gospels: (See also Matthew 16:25; Mark 8:35; Luke 9:24 and 17:35; John 12:25). In that spirit, Esther understands she is not free to live her life until she accepts its boundaries and limitations. The meaning of her death overrides the meaning of her life. Her life is not hers to claim until she is able to renounce it.

Esther faces death with integrity, not with despair. Her life has not been in vain…the cause is worthy, it is worth her life. Jesus manifested a similar spirit when he said, "Greater love has no man than this, that he lay down his life for his friends" (John 15:13) Esther was willing to lay her life down for her people. Arguably, she is the only person in the Old Testament willing to offer her life in a manner similar to that of Jesus of Nazareth in the New Testament. If Esther were contemporary short fiction, she would be called a Christ-figure.

QUESTIONS FOR STUDY AND DISCUSSION

1. What situations of injustice and threats to the well-being of specific groups of people have you witnessed? How have you responded?

2. Who are some of the heroes throughout American history that you revere for their courageous efforts to stop injustice? What actions made them heroes in your mind?

3. If people of faith do not voice their opposition when minority groups are singled out for ridicule or persecution, how will God's voice be heard and heeded?

4. What is the main message you have received from the study of the Book of Esther? How will new insights from this study affect the way you live and witness to your faith?

5. Besides the Holocaust of World War II, what other parallels can you draw in world history? In the history of the United States?

6. What are the underlying causes of genocide, or the annihilation of an entire race or ethnic group by another?

Chapter Ten

Jonah

THE TEXT

The word of the Lord came to Jonah son of Amittai: "Go to the city of Nineveh and preach against it, because its wickedness has come up before me. But Jonah ran away from the Lord and headed for Tarshish. He went down to Joppa, where he found a ship bound for that port . . . . Then the Lord sent a great wind on the sea, such a violent storm arose that the ship threatened to break up. All the sailors were afraid and each cried out to his own god...Then the sailors said to each other, "come let us cast lots to find out who is responsible for this calamity . . . and the lot fell on Jonah . . . . "What should we do to you to make the sea calm down for us?" "Pick me up and throw me into the sea," he replied, "and it will become calm. I know that it is my fault that this great storm has come upon you." . . . Then they took Jonah and threw him overboard and the raging sea grew calm . . . . But the Lord provided a great fish to swallow Jonah and Jonah was inside the fish three days and three nights . . . . And the Lord commanded the fish, and it vomited Jonah onto dry ground.

—Jonah 1:1-3, 4, 7, 11-12, 15, 17

Then the word of the Lord came to Jonah a second time: "Go
to the city of Nineveh and proclaim to it the message I give
you." Jonah obeyed the word of the Lord and went to
Nineveh . . . . The Ninevites believed God.

—Jonah 3:1-3, 5

But Jonah was greatly displeased and became angry . . . . But
the Lord replied, "Have you any right to be angry?"

—Jonah 4:1, 4

THE CONTEXT

The *Book of Jonah* is the fifth of the Minor Prophets in the Old
Testament. The book is unique among the books of prophets because it
tells a story *about* a prophet rather than expressing the
pronouncements of a prophet. Over time the story has been regarded as
history, parable, allegory, fairy tale, fable, myth, sermon and satire. It
is a coherent narrative with many diverse elements, all stemming from
rich and varying traditions. The problem with calling *Jonah* a history
is less about the incredulous story of a man reaching the belly of a fish
intact than about other actions of the story. The reader is asked to
believe that **the raging sea grew calm** (1:15) immediately when Jonah
was thrown overboard, and that he wrote a psalm of thanksgiving
while inside the fish for three days, and then was coughed up on a
beach uninjured by the fish. These, and other aspects of the story, have
been challenging over the generations but are particularly difficult for
people of faith in the 21st century.

Using the allegory label, each feature of the story represents an
element of Israel's experience. "Jonah" means a "dove," a traditional
symbol of Israel (Pslam 74:19, Hosea 11:11). The experiences of the
prophet represent the mission and failure of Israel to be the people of
God and to bring the pagan world to the knowledge of God. Scholars
agree that the story is about Israel represented by Jonah. His peril in
the storm at sea is a metaphor for the history of Israel. If the story was

written relatively late, the readers of that era would see the symbols of their national destruction and despair, their banishment to an alien land, and their pining away in exile. All of this happens to Jonah, and in the end he is upset and angry because God forgives a city of a foreign non-Hebrew land. Some scholars agree that Israel's national death and resurrection is expressed in the psalm of Chapter 2.

Efforts at dating the composition of Jonah have proven elusive. The story reflects no particular historical setting. Because of a reference in 2 Kings to a Jonah, son of Amittai in the reign of Jeroboam II, some scholars have chosen the 8th century BCE. However, the *Book of Jonah* is mentioned in the *Wisdom of ben Sira* (49:10) which would infer a 2nd century BCE date. Most scholars agree the book was written sometime between those time frames. In other words, it may be pre-exilic or post-exilic. Along with the uncertainty of its genre, setting, date of composition and place of origin, the purpose of the book is equally unknown.

The story, presented in two related halves, begins abruptly, without any historical background or introduction. In the first half, Jonah is in the ship with the sailors and their captain. In the second part, he is in Nineveh with the Ninevites and their king. Each scene opens with **"Now the word of the Lord came to Jonah . . . ."**(1:1; 3:1)

The focal point of the narrative has become Jonah's sojourn in the belly of the fish, an event which is a minor detail in the major thrust of the story. The primary theme is about a psychologically complex man fleeing God and disobeying his word. The main characters, Jonah and God, appear in each scene. The hero is not Jonah, but God. Other nameless characters emerge from leaderless groups. In Shakespearean fashion, natural elements—wind, storm, sea, dry land, and fish in scene one; animals, plant, worm, sun, and wind in scene two—play key roles. The plot moves along and turns on human and natural responses to divine intervention.

Jonah resists God's call which is not unique in Old Testament. Moses resisted the call at the burning bush. (Exodus 3:10-4:17) Elijah resisted from criticizing the regime of Ahab. (1 Kings 19:1-18) Jeremiah resisted prophesying to the nations, (Jeremiah 1:4-10) But none is more defiant than Jonah who exemplifies blatant disobedience. Jonah not only flees the divine presence, he rejects the divine call.

The Story

The outline of *Jonah* is simple:

> Chapter 1: The story of the sailors delivered from the storm at sea with two parts: 1) Jonah's "Great Refusal" and 2) his punishment.
> Chapter 2: Jonah is swallowed and vomited by a fish at sea.
> Chapter 3: The Ninevites are saved from the threat of destruction.
> Chapter 4: A discussion between Jonah and God

The plot of *Jonah* centers on a conflict between Jonah and God. God calls Jonah to go to Nineveh and pronounce judgment on the city and its people. Jonah resists and tries to flee God's presence. He goes first to Joppa, an Israeli coastal city. He pays full fare and boards a ship bound for Tarshish, presumably a city in Spain at the other end of the world. The full fare and the location indicate Jonah's desperation to permanently escape God. God creates a mighty storm at sea. The ship's crew cast lots to determine the cause and throw Jonah overboard to appease God. A great sea creature, possibly a whale, is sent by God and swallows Jonah. For three days and three nights, Jonah sojourns inside the belly of the fish. While inside the fish's belly he utters a prayer. He repents for his disobedience and asks God for mercy. God causes the fish to vomit Jonah safely onto dry land. Following his rescue, Jonah obeys God's call to prophesy against Nineveh. Led by the king, the inhabitants put on sackcloth, repent, and are forgiven by God. In an ironic twist, the persistent and unyielding God of the first chapter becomes the merciful God in the last two chapters. Parallel to that irony, Jonah becomes a successful prophet by turning all of the inhabitants of Nineveh to God.

In the fourth chapter, despite this great success, Jonah becomes distraught and despairs to the point of wanting to die. He perches on a hilltop beneath a vine where he can see the city and watches, hoping God will still destroy it. But Jonah had another lesson to learn. While in a state of deep depression, Jonah receives a sharp rebuke from God. In essence, God accuses Jonah of being overly concerned with the vine, which he did not grow, but shows no concern for the people of

Nineveh. Jonah's egotism and selfishness are revealed. The story ends as abruptly as it began with a question: **Should I not be concerned about that great city?** (4:11b)

THE MESSAGE

1:1-2—The word of the Lord came to Jonah son of Amittal:

"Go to the great city of Nineveh and preach against it."

Jonah was sailing along in life, probably successful (he had money to pay a full fare), accomplished, building toward his retirement, having occasional visits with friends. Then God called and suddenly everything was turned upside down. In this case God's call was clear, unambiguous, and definite: **' . . . arise, go to Nineveh, that great city, and cry out against it; for their wickedness has come up before me'**

When God calls us, we might resist as Moses did. We might be fearful as Abraham, not knowing where he was going. But would we flee?

Perhaps we no longer hear God's call. "It may not be the case that God no longer speaks to modern people. Rather, it may be the case that modern people like you and me are no longer listening, are no longer obeying or responding to the voice of God."[116]

1:3—But Jonah ran away from the Lord and headed for Tarshish. He went down to Joppa where he found a ship bound for that port. After paying the fare he went aboard and sailed for Tarshish to flee from the Lord.

But Jonah ran away from the Lord. The story of Jonah does not raise the question about hearing God. Jonah heard God loud and clear. If we heard that definite and clear voice, would we pretend we did not hear and avoid its response? Do we turn away and seek refuge in work, play, addictions, unhealthy relationships, immerse ourselves in so much "stuff" we pretend we do not hear. If so, we are like Jonah. We are *running* away. Perhaps we leave town for a while, take a vacation, move to another location, all with the hoped for effect that the word will be left behind, die down, cease. The

Book of Jonah says, "It won't happen." It points to the futility in trying to avoid or escape God's word.

The often quoted ode "Hound of Heaven" by Francis Thompson is as relevant to this issue now as it was to its readers of the 1890's:

> I fled Him down the nights and down the days;
>
> I fled Him down the arches of the years;
>
> I fled Him down the labyrinthine ways
>
> Of my own mind, and in the midst of tears
>
> I hid from Him, and under running laughter.[117]

The words from the writer of the 139th Psalm are as fresh and alive now as they were when sung and written millennia ago:

> Where can I go from your Spirit?
>
> Where can I flee from your presence?
>
> If I go up to the heavens, you are there;
>
> if I make my bed in the depths, you are there.
>
> If I rise on the wings of the dawn.
>
> if I settle on the far side of the sea,
>
> even there your hand will guide me,
>
> your right hand will hold me fast. (vv7-10)

Jonah's inability to escape God is also reflected in Psalms (65:5-7; 107:23-32; 139:7-12, cf. also Jeremiah 23:19-20.)

God never gives up. His search is relentless. This point emerges in Jesus' *Parable of the Lost Sheep*. In the *Gospel of Luke* the Pharisees have protested that a man "welcomes sinners and eats with them" (15:2) Then Jesus tells the parable about the joy in heaven over one lost sinner who repents compared to ninety-nine righteous persons who need no repentance. God rejoices because he forgives. A sub-theme of the parable is the shepherd's relentless search until he finds the sheep. Both themes apply to the Jonah story. The people of Nineveh are lost and need to repent. Paradoxically, Jonah is the lost sheep relentlessly hounded by God to go and save them. God then rejoices over the saved city and Jonah pouts on a hill overlooking the city. (Jonah 4:5).

How many of us share Jonah's naivety, his shallow theology? When have we tried to escape God's Word, His commandments, His strong moral code? When have we shut our ears and eyes and tried not to hear or see, to negate His presence enveloping us, following us wherever we go? We might do well to think about the last crisis in our life, the last "wake-up" call reminding us of our dependency upon a higher power, our connection to the Creator. God gets to Jonah through a storm. For some of us, it takes a storm, some terrible conflict or crisis or tragedy to enable us to feel God's presence.

In his book *Alone,* Admiral Richard Byrd tells of an experience in which he was trapped in a white-out, an arctic phenomenon that obliterates all sense of direction. Grown men and women become totally lost and fall to their knees groping for a familiar object that is perhaps inches from their fingertips. Byrd said the first emotion that washed over him was total fear. Minutes passed and another emotion, anger, took over. He wanted to strike out at whatever force had made him so helpless. A longer time passed and he said he encountered a third feeling, that of a Presence. Similar to Admiral Byrd and Jonah, it takes a storm for some to feel God's presence. New Testament parallels of escape to the sea followed by a storm then moments of faith are found in Mark 4:1, 35-41; Matthew 8:24-27; Acts 27. Unfortunately, Judas, in his flight, never encountered that experience.

1:7—Then they said to each other, "Come, let us cast lots to find out who is responsible for this calamity." They cast lots and the lot fell on Jonah.

The sailors are innocent uninvolved victims in this conflict. They happen to be passengers on a ship with a man rebelling against God. In this verse the issue of the suffering of innocents is raised. Why do bad things happen to innocent people?

Jonah's conflict with God draws others into the fray. Jonah is concerned with only one objective, defying God, not saving the sailors. His sole focus, his egoism and self-centered agenda, embroils and endangers others. Jonah presents as selfish, obsessed, and obstinate: "It's my way or no way." He wallows in self-pity. He even mocks God by calling Him Creator as he flees his presence.

Rebellion against God is rarely an isolated act. Inevitably, others become sucked into the conflict. When we disobey the laws of Creation and the ethics of Christ, innocent people are injured. The children of relationships do not ask to be drawn into their parents' quarrels, but they necessarily become caught up in the bitterness and hostility that often leads to divorce and the shattering of their small innocent lives. The poor and downtrodden of third world countries have no say in the wars their leaders declare, yet they are the ones who suffer the most. The citizens of developed countries, like the United States, have little influence in their leader's decisions to invade another country, yet in the long run, they pay the price.

1:17—But the Lord provided a great fish to swallow Jonah who was inside the fish three days and three nights.

Despite all of his machinations and plans, God saved Jonah from the storm. God will find a way to save us, regardless of our efforts to betray His goodness and love. The path of salvation may be tough and filled with pain not of our choosing, but we ultimately trust that, "in all things God works for the good of those who love him, who have been called according to his purpose" (Romans 8:28). As Jonah was loved and called, we are loved and have been called. Regardless of our choices, our behavior, or our thoughts, God can save us in all situations.

Some may say of *Jonah*, "It's just a story." There are stories in the Bible that seem to be, "just a story," which was one of the reasons for writing this book. Like the stories of creation, the Flood, Tower of Babel and David and Goliath, the story of Jonah about a storm at sea and a big fish is true in the mythological sense. It is "a true story" in that it is a true depiction of the nature of a God who uses every means possible to get at us, to get through to those who are the objects of his love. God is seeking not only Jonah but the people of Nineveh. He is determined that they hear of his justice and mercy. He has also decided that Jonah, despite his faults, is an instrument of divine mercy. God's will is not easily derailed.

One possible interpretation of Jonah's descent into the belly of the whale is symbolic of those who struggle with God's call. More obvious than the symbolic meaning of the fish's belly is the reason Jonah descended there in the first place: his egoism. A direct association between selfishness and destructiveness is Jonah's egotistic behavior that placed him in his predicament.

2:1-10—Jonah's prayer in the belly of the fish

Jonah's egoism becomes full blown in the bowels of the fish.
The psalm, or prayer, he recites is a contradiction. Jonah prays thanksgiving yet uses the personal pronoun "I" 26 times.[1] The prayer revolves around him and what happened to him and includes boastful phraseology. The psalm is an example of the vicious cycle of self-centeredness that leads to suffering and to self-pity and generates egoism.

3:1-2—Then the word of the Lord came to Jonah a second time: "Go to the great city of Nineveh and proclaim to it the message I give you.

As noted in the "Introduction," the hero in the story is not Jonah, but God. Similar to the Parable of the Prodigal Son, the story of Jonah is about God's character, his persistence. When we turn from God, or run away to a far country, God's love and care do not cease nor does He not turn from us.

Despite Jonah's elaborate plans to escape God, God still calls, and Jonah hears. These verses reflect the persistence of the Divine call, a persistence that wears down opposition. Though the context is different, the reader might recall the *Parable of the Unjust Judge* (Luke 18:1-8). According to Joachim Jeremias, the parable is about the persistence of prayer. The widow's persistence with the judge is her only weapon. In his interpretation Jeremias states, "If this inconsiderate man, who has been refusing to hear the widow's case, finally gives heed to her distress, how much more will the will of God! God listens to the cry of the poor with unwearied patience."[118] In the story of Jonah, the roles are reversed. God's "unwearied patience" is a major theme and in the end, God prevails.

3:5—The Ninevites believed God.

Regardless of the source, God respects true repentance. This truth is represented many times in the parables of Jesus, particularly the *Parable of the Prodigal Son.* God's love for all creation, all peoples, and all nations is difficult for Jonah, an Israelite, one of God's chosen to accept. He resents having to go to the ungodly because they do not deserve God's grace or love, and especially his forgiveness. But God can act benevolently toward other nations, not just Israel. This God is bigger than Jonah thought. Jesus would echo this later: "I have other sheep that are not of this sheep pen" (John 10:16)

This story mirrors an attitude prevalent in our own nation. Like Jonah's opinion of Nineveh, many tend to think America is a piece of God's real estate and the rest of the world is pagan. But the message in Jonah is God's love for all the world, for all people. In crisis situations, Christians, Jews, and Muslims all need God's mercy. In all lands— Baghdad, Tehran, North Korean, and beyond—people are of God's creation and they all qualify for his mercy and forgiveness. According to God's word, this message is axiomatic, a given.

The conversion of an entire city in one fell swoop might raise a brow. Mass conversions are often suspect of being emotionally manipulated and thus superficial. On the other hand, faith can work within systems, within entire political bodies. God's word prevails despite the conditions of a system. The mission programs of many congregations thrive despite the handicap, ineptness, or immoral behavior of a pastor or the lack of vision of their governing bodies. "The wind blows wherever it pleases" (John 3:8).

**4:1, 4—But Jonah was greatly displeased and became angry . . . .
But the Lord replied, "Have you any right to be angry?"**

Anger results in destruction. The direction of self-will is always away from God and leads to personal destruction. God does not denigrate or condemn Jonah for being angry. Instead, as a good therapist, God tries to help Jonah work through his anger. He encourages Jonah to reflect on the meaning of his anger. Jonah needs to understand that his anger comes from within. Anger is often symptomatic of a deeper underlying depression. Much depression is the result of self-centeredness. Simply put, when we do not get our way, we often pout, become depressed and manifest the depression as anger. "Psychologically, Jonah's anger manifests narcissism; theologically, it bespeaks egotism."[119] Jonah is wrestling with himself. Anger is symptomatic of that depressed struggle. His ego refuses to submit to a higher Will.

4:5-8—Jonah went out and sat down at a place east of the city. There he made himself a shelter, sat in the shade and waited to see what would happen to the city. Then the Lord provided a vine and made it grow to give . . . Jonah shade . . . . Jonah was very happy about the vine. But at dawn . . . God provided a worm which chewed the vine. When the sun rose . . . a scorching east wind, and the sun blazed on Jonah's head so he grew faint and wanted to die, and said, "It would be better for me to die than to live."

The pattern of Jonah's passive behavior continues. With the exception of buying ship fare and climbing aboard, Jonah has been passive. He has been incapable of taking action. He asks the sailors to throw him overboard. He asks God to end his life. He sits on a hill waiting to see what will happen to the city. Passive behavior is the perfect strategy for depression so there is little wonder Jonah's depression finds an outlet in his anger.

The author mentions **"The city"** twice in verse five, offering a sharp contrast with the solitary, lonely and depressed figure sitting on a nearby hill. Through his own stubborn and selfish behavior, Jonah has shut himself out of the city. God provides him a shelter then takes the shelter away. At one time, Israel was prosperous then its prosperity disappeared. Did its national inward self-righteous focus cause the demise? Israel has experienced God's grace numerous times but still calls on the Almighty to destroy its foes. Many scholars see in this story a parable of Israel's fate by piously clinging to its purity of law and religion.

4:10, 11b—But the Lord said… "Should I not be concerned about that city?

Jonah had been so obsessed with his protection from the noon day sun, he had lost concern for the ultimate goal, the city. Through this last question, God compares Jonah's narrow-mindedness with that of the teeming unfortunate people in the city. God has compassion for the multitudes of the city . . . **a hundred and twenty thousand people who cannot tell their right hand from their left . . . ."**(4:11). Of the few times Jesus is recorded as weeping, one was over the city. In this passage the writer describes a compassionate God who is concerned with all of creation which includes the teeming urban masses. "Jonah stands as an ever-present reminder of the perils of ignoring the will of God. In Jonah's day, God was determined to be merciful even to those who were bitter enemies of His Chosen People. Jonah resisted such boundless mercy and fled from the will of God."[120]

Upon reaching the end of the story where Jonah is left sitting on the hill pouting, the reader begins to get the point: "The reader is Jonah . . . so the open-endedness of the last verse invites self-understanding and self-transcendence. The story subverts the reader."[121] One final statement from Gerhard von Radd serves as a fitting conclusion to the commentary: "It is worth noticing that one of the last utterances of Israelite prophecy is so devastatingly self-critical; for in the way in which in this Book it strips itself of all honor, and turns men's gaze away from itself in order to give the honor to him to whom alone this is due, it reveals something of the 'he must increase, but I must decrease' spoken by the last in the line of these ambassadors (Jn. III, 30)."[122]

QUESTIONS FOR FURTHER STUDY AND DISCUSSION

1. What does this incredulous story mean? How can it convey any meaning to the 21st century believer?
2. What are the primary lessons to be learned from this story?
3. In what ways is this story a metaphor of situations in the 21st century? Where are the parallels?
4. What is the value of anger? What are the results/outcome of anger? What are the solutions for anger?
5. In this story who emerges as the most righteous and why?

Chapter Eleven

Daniel

THE TEXT

But Daniel resolved not to defile himself with the royal food and wine, and he asked the chief official for permission not to defile himself this way . . . . Daniel then said to the guard . . . "Please test your servants for ten days."

At the end of ten days . . . the king talked with them, and he found none equal to Daniel, Hananiah, Mishael and Azariah . . . .

—Daniel 1:8,11,19

The King asked Daniel, "are you able to tell me what I saw in my dream and interpret it?"

Daniel replied, no wise man, enchanter, magician or diviner can explain to the king the mystery he has asked about, but there is a God in heaven who reveals mysteries."

—Daniel 2:26-28

Then King Nebuchanezzar leaped to his feet in amazement and asked his advisors, "Weren't there three men that we tied up and threw into the fire?"

They replied, "Certainly, O king."

He said, "Look! I see four men walking around in the fire…"

—Daniel 3:24-25

Suddenly the fingers of a human hand appeared and wrote on the plaster of the wall . . . . The king watched the hand as it wrote. His face turned pale and he was so frightened that his knees knocked together and his legs gave way . . . . This is the inscription that was written: MENE, MENE, TEKEL, PARSIN.

—Daniel 5:5-6, 25

At the first light of dawn, the king got up and hurried to the lions' den. When he came near the den, he called to Daniel in an anguished voice, "Daniel, servant of the living God, has your god . . . been able to rescue you from the lions?" Daniel answered, "O, king, live forever. My God sent his angel and shut the mouths of the lions. They have not hurt me because I was found innocent in his sight."

—Daniel 6:19-21

In my vision at night I looked, and there before me was one like a son of man, coming with the clouds of heaven. He approached the Ancient of Days and was led into his presence. He was given authority, glory and sovereign, all peoples, nations and men of every language worshipped him. His dominion is an everlasting dominion that will not pass away, and his kingdom is one that will never be destroyed.

—Daniel 7:13-14

THE CONTEXT

The *Book of Daniel* is placed with "The Writings" in the Hebrew Old Testament but included with the Prophets in the Christian Old Testament. Though no names are mentioned, people and events are easily identified. These include Antiochus IV Epiphanes of Syria and the persecution of the Jews, which began in 168 B.C. The book, dated by most scholars to the time of the Maccabean Revolt, is well-known in the *Dead Sea Scrolls* and also found in a range of other Jewish writings not included in the Bible. Bernard Anderson dates the composition shortly after the outbreak of the Maccabean wars and attributes authorship to an Hasidic Jew. The Hasidim, also known as "Pious Ones," a conservative branch of Judaism, were men of piety devoted to prayer and study of the Torah. This orthodox group was outraged and disgusted by the imposition of Hellenism on their religion and their culture and the accompanying tyranny of Antiochus IV Epiphanes. The Jewish faith, in the writer's opinion, was in danger of extinction by the policies of the Seleucids and he wrote *Daniel* as an alarm and summons to his people to remain loyal to their God and their faith during this time of persecution. For this reason the book has been called "The Manifesto of the Hasidim."[123]

Daniel is a form of apocalyptic literature usually written in times of persecution. It is filled with strange visions, unusual symbolism, supernatural beings and occurrences, and written in a form of secret code that makes it a "sealed book." (Daniel12:4) The primary theme is God's revelations concerning the end of time, or *eschaton*, and the coming of His Kingdom. Chapters seven through twelve, narrated in the first person, are apocalyptic revelations. The word apocalypse (from the Greek *apokalypsis*) means "unveiling" or "revealing."[124] Apocalyptic literature is mysterious revealed wisdom which has an *immediate* relation to redemption. The best known example of apocalyptic literature is the *Book of Revelation* in the New Testament. The genre was represented in the Old Testament by the *Book of Daniel.*[125]

The *Book of Daniel* is a prime example of Jewish Apocalypticism that arose about 200 to 250 years before Jesus of Nazareth in a time of great suffering among the Jewish people. In Daniel and the *Enoch* series is the first mention of the apocalyptic figure "son of man," a term Jesus often used and many avow is a reference to himself. Daniel also contains other biblical firsts: the first mention of the kingdom of God and first reference to the resurrection of the dead.

The intent of the writer(s) of Daniel was to offer hope and consolation to the Jewish people in the midst of persecution. The resulting apocalyptic theology unfolded with an interesting logic: This punishment of the Jewish people could not come from God. It must come from another source, such as cosmic evil or cosmic powers or forces of evil. Therefore, this material evil world must not be a creation of the one true God who is All Good. Some other god, who is beneath God the Creator, had a hand in it. At some point in the future, God will intervene and overthrow this god and his evil powers. Victory will be achieved at the hands of the Archangel Michael and the martyrs will be rewarded with resurrection.[126] In other words, the revered God of the Hebrews is relieved of any responsibility for evil.

The *Book of Daniel* is divided into two parts. The first, chapters one through six, comprise a collection of court stories, teaching narratives, and miracle legends all set at the Babylonian and Persian courts and narrated in the third person. The second part, chapters seven through twelve are apocalyptic revelations through Daniel's visions and narrated in the first person.

The Story

Part 1: The Narratives

Following their capture and trek to Babylon, members of the Israelite elite and nobility are inducted into the king's service. To avoid defiling their bodies, Daniel and his three friends Hananiah, Mishael, and Azariah decline the king's food and wine. Following a brief trial period they appear healthier than their Gentile trainees who have been eating food allowed by the king and are permitted to continue on their diet. After three years, Daniel and his three friends are brought before the king who finds them, **ten times better than all**

the magicians and enchanters in his whole kingdom (1:20). Daniel remains in the king's service until the reign of Cyrus.

The focus of chapter two is Nebuchadnezzar's dream where he sees an idol constructed of four metals. A rock destroys the idol then rules the world. The king's wise men are unable to interpret his dream. Daniel interprets the metallic composition as representative of four successive empires that are destroyed by the kingdom of God.

In chapter three, the king builds a towering gold statue and orders his subjects to bow to the idol. Hananiah, Mishael, and Azariah (their names are changed to Shadrach, Meshach, and Abednego) refuse to bow to the golden statue. As a result, the men are thrown into the furnace but they survive. Upon seeing another figure with the three in the furnace the king makes his famous statement, **Weren't there three men that we tied up and threw into the furnace** (3:24b). The king gives credit and praise to the men's **Most High God.**

In chapter four Nebuchadnezzar has another dream in which a huge tree is suddenly felled at the orders of a divine messenger. Again the king's wise men fail to interpret the dream and again Daniel is summonsed. Daniel explains that for seven years Nebuchadnezzar will lose power and turn into a beast. When the dream becomes reality, Nebuchadnezzar recognizes the supremacy of heaven and his kingdom and sanity are restored.

The next event, a feast given by Belshazzar, shows his nobles drinking sacrilegiously from Jewish temple vessels and praising their own gods. **Suddenly the fingers of a human hand appeared and wrote on the. plaster of the wall . . . MENE, MENE TEKEL, UPHARSIN.** (5:5, 25) Daniel is summonsed and provides the following interpretation. **MENE** means God numbers the days of Belshazzar's reign. **TEKEL** means Belshazzar has been found guilty on the scales of justice, and **UPHARSIN** divides Belshazzar's kingdom between the Medes and Persians. **That very night Belshazzar, king of the Babylonians was slain, and Darius the Mede took over the kingdom at the age of sixty-two.** (5:30)

Under the rule of "Darius," Daniel ascends to a prominent position and reaps the jealousy of other officials. To gain revenge, they trick the king into ordering an edict prohibiting worship to any god or human for thirty days. Daniel continues facing Jerusalem three times daily and praying. He is accused of disobeying the king's edict and thrown into the lions' den. Upon finding him unharmed the next morning, the king orders his accusers and their families cast into the lions' den, and they are immediately eaten.

Part 2: The Apocalyptic Visions

Chapters six through twelve are apocalyptic and visionary. The voice now changes to the first person as Daniel describes the visions provided only to him. In this segment, heavenly figures serve as interpreters of the visions.

The first vision occurs in the first year of the reign of Belshazzar, king of Babylon. In a dream, Daniel sees four great beasts rise from the sea, the **Ancient of Days** on his throne, and **one like a son of man coming with the clouds of heaven** (7:13). An angel explains the four beasts represent four future kings or kingdoms that will be destroyed. The fourth beast, described as having ten horns representing ten kingdoms, consumes the entire earth and crushes it. The last person arising from the fourth kingdom conquers three of the ten kings (7:24), orates against the Most High and the saints of the Most High, and pronounces his intention of changing the law (7:25). This person, according to the vision, will be judged, his kingdom removed from him, **Then the sovereignty, power and greatness of the kingdoms under the whole heaven will be handed over to the saints, the people of the Most High. His kingdom will be an everlasting kingdom and rulers will worship and obey him** (7:27).

In Belshazzar's third year, the second vision occurs featuring a ram and a male goat symbolic of Medo-Persia and Greece. The focus of the vision is a wicked king who rises up to challenge **the mighty men and the holy people** by removing the daily temple sacrifice and desecrating the sanctuary for **2300 evenings and mornings** (8:14).

The vision in the first year of Darius, the son of Ahasuerus, is about a meditation based upon the prediction in Jeremiah that the desolation of Jerusalem would last seventy years. In a lengthy prayer, Daniel pleads for God to restore Jerusalem and its temple. His prayer is followed by Gabriel's explanation projecting a longer time period –

"seventy sevens." His explanation also includes the prediction of the destruction of Jerusalem and the Temple by a future ruler.

The final vision occurs in the third year of Cyrus king of Persia. The focus is on conflicts between the "King of the North" and the "King of the South." Mentioning Persia and Greece again, the vision concludes with a description of a contemptible and deceitful king who desecrates the temple, removes the daily sacrifice, **sets up the abomination that causes desolation,** and **corrupt those who have violated the covenant.** (11:31-32) There will be great distress among the people, but they will be delivered.

THE MESSAGE

Note: Due to the structure of the *Book of Daniel,* **The Message** section focuses on key chapters.

Daniel 1:1-21

The first chapter of *Daniel* could be entitled "A Test of Character." Daniel's character was tested when he was thrown into the lions' den, a story most of us know from childhood. But, his mettle was also tested when he was a teenager on the seemingly innocuous and unimportant issues of food and drink. Daniel and his companions were assigned a daily ration of **food and wine from the king's table**, a diet most of us would be happy to have. But, they declined and requested **nothing but vegetables to eat and water to drink** (1:12)

The **food and wine from the king's table** was tempting to Daniel and his companions following a long trek. They were in a strange land and they missed their homeland and its familiar food, drink, and tastes. Food from the king's kitchen would meet a basic human need, but did not uphold their spiritual convictions that included religion and diet. For the Jew of faith, food laws were a major issue. Jews could eat only kosher foods. Pork, beef, or camel that had been sacrificed to another god were forbidden. Eating and drinking may seem insignificant to us in the 21st century, but eating **food and wine from the king's table** would compromise Daniel's faith. So **Daniel resolved not to defile himself.**

David O. Dykes reminds us that, "The word *diet* originally meant more than the food one consumed: it described an individual's way of life, encompassing his or her emotional, spiritual, social, and physical dimensions."[127] This definition also recalls the original definition of the word "holy," a healthy, wholesome, integrated personality. Daniel was focused on the original meaning of the word, but he may also have been attuned to the ancients' view of personality known today as "holistic medicine." For Daniel, the spiritual component of the word *diet* was significant. It was important that he follow God's plan.

Not only were questions about diet and dietary laws frequently raised in the New Testament and in early Christianity, they were a serious threat within the church. Because early Christianity was basically a Jewish reform movement, many early Christians continued to practice their Levitical diet. Jesus must have been an embarrassment to some of his Jewish contemporaries. He is described as eating and drinking with tax-collectors, publicans, and sinners (Matthew 9:11; Mark 2:16; Luke 5:30; 7:34), behavior considered anathema to pious Jews. He was succinct in his comments about diet and ritual uncleanness. When he and his disciples were criticized by Pharisees for eating food with "unclean" hands, he retorted, "Nothing outside a man can make him 'unclean' by going into him. Rather, it is what comes out of a man that makes him 'unclean.'" The writer of Mark states parenthetically, "In saying this, Jesus declared all foods 'clean.'" (7:19; cf. Luke 11:47). In Acts, Peter receives a vision in which he sees "a large sheet...containing all kinds of four-footed, as well as reptiles of the earth and birds of the air," then a voice tells him, "Get up, Peter, kill and eat." (10:11-13) Peter says that he has never eaten anything "unclean," and the voice responds again, "Do not call anything impure that God has made clean." (10:15) The issue of Jewish food laws, however, continued to be a point of contention (Cf. Galatians2:11-13 and Colossians 2:16). A compromise solution was finally instituted at the Council of Jerusalem where it was decided that Christians were to, "abstain from food sacrificed to idols, from blood, from the meat of strangled animals and from sexual immorality." (Acts 15:29). Paul added his own formula to the debate: "...no food is unclean in itself. But if anyone regards something as unclean, then for him it is unclean. If your brother is distressed because of what you eat, you are no longer acting in love. Do not by your eating destroy your brother for whom Christ died…For the kingdom of God is not a matter of eating and drinking. But of righteousness, peace, and joy in the Holy Spirit" (Romans 14:14-15, 17). This position is developed by Paul more fully in 1 Corinthians 10.

The issue mentioned above in these New Testament passages is different from that found in the story of Daniel where the concern is loyalty of these young men to their God. The New Testament message of Jesus and Paul focuses on the spirit, not the letter, of the law. Spiritual authority and matters of the spirit super-cede legal requirements.

As Christians, we live in a complex and multifaceted culture that daily encroaches upon our values and spiritual identity. The **food and wine from the king's table** are symbolic of the things we must resist in order to maintain the values and loyalty to Christ and the gospel. Christians living in Iran, Iraq, and other fundamentalist Islamic Shiite countries will relate immediately to this message. The writer of the *Book of Daniel* used food and wine as symbols reflecting deeper issues, namely the assimilation of Jewish people, their culture and religion, into a foreign culture. In Islamic Shiite countries the code of dress is important. This same issue surfaces in our own country regarding dress code, outside the realm of religion. Children become segregated, excluded, because they do not dress like others or wear designer clothes. Being a minority and standing by your values and customs is difficult in the 21st century as it was for Daniel.

Daniel resisted the king's food and wine. Symbolically and literally, what are the king's food and wine that we must resist? We must distinguish between the things that are necessary and unnecessary. Food is a necessity, but we tend to elevate unnecessary things to the same level with food. In the last century, John Kenneth Galbreath coined a phrase, "consumer demand creation."[128] This simply meant that the advertising industry had successfully enticed the American consumers to develop a false sense of need that resulted in becoming self-indulged and over-indulged, partially through a trick of psychology. The recent financial crisis has caused many to take a second look, regroup, and become more disciplined. Like Daniel, they are refusing to partake of the **king's food and wine** and are establishing goals, agendas, and expectations more realistically geared to a life of self-control and discipline. The results are healthier budgets and diets and a less indulgent life-style. Rick Warren, the author of *The Purpose Driven Life* has a new purpose. He recruited a number of prominent physicians, including Dr. Mehmer Oz of The Dr. Oz Show, and together they developed *The Daniel Plan: God's Prescription for Your Health.* The plan encourages fitness and diet and encourages church members to join groups for support.

Daniel served as a positive role model by refusing to eat food that had probably been grown by the poor and given as a tax to the monarchy. Likewise, some Americans are becoming more discriminating about a product's market and are refusing to buy items made by child or slave labor.

Food is a necessity but nutritional foods are essential for maintaining healthy bodies. Based on the king's indulgent lifestyle, his diet was likely filled with the types of food our doctors tell us today to avoid or limit. Daniel's request for vegetables indicates he was eating some of the healthiest foods available. Even as a teenager, Daniel was making healthy choices by following the Levitic law of his religion. Within days, he and his companions appeared healthier than the trainees who had been eating and drinking from the king's store.

Our body is a holy temple, (1 Corinthians 6:19; cf. also 1 Corinthians 3:16-17) and Paul reminds us to treat our bodies with great care because they are sacred. If we are among the fortunate who do not have health issues, we want to prevent them. Daniel serves as a positive example of discipline in avoiding the foods and drinks that defile and pollute our body.

Daniel is also a paragon of loyalty to his faith. For Daniel and his companions, maintaining their faith was not a formula for success. They understood and were willing to accept, the consequences. The *Book of Job* demonstrates clearly that right belief and righteous behavior do not guarantee immunity from trials and suffering. Esther said, "I if I perish, I perish."(4:15b) The theology of "believe and prosper" is not the theology of the Savior who said, "Take up your cross and follow me."

Daniel 2:1-49

On the surface, chapter two of *Daniel* focuses primarily on the meaning and interpretation of a dream that was troubling Nebuchadnezzar. The content of the dream is not as important as the deaths it caused, the pressure it placed upon Daniel, and how he dealt with that pressure. The astrologers and wise men who were unable to interpret the dream were executed. Daniel was called to perform the impossible.

"God will never put more on you than you can bear," is a statement designed to encourage, but is faulty theology. The opposite of this statement is biblically true. Throughout the Bible, we read of individuals upon whom God does place unbearable burdens. At that point, they turn to the Lord and trust in His strength. In his vulnerability, Daniel depended on God and not on his own resources. Paul echoes this theme in 2 Corinthians: "We do not want you to be uninformed, brothers, about the hardships we suffered in the province of Asia. We were under great pressure, far beyond our ability to endure, so that we despaired even of life. Indeed, in our hearts we felt the sentence of death. But this happened that we might not rely on ourselves but on God, who raises the dead. He has delivered us from such a deadly peril, and he will deliver us." (1:8-10).

Before taking any action, Daniel prayed. (2:20-23). The importance of prayer to Daniel surfaces again in this book (6:10-11; 9:4-21) and underscores its critical role in his life. For Daniel, prayer was a first option, not a final resort. The writer of the New Testament *Book of James* might have read Daniel prior to penning the opening of his epistle and this strategy of prayer: "If any of you lacks wisdom, he should ask God, who gives generously to all without finding fault, and it will be given to him" (1:5). The writer of Ephesians echoes this confidence: "Now to him who is able, to do immeasurably more than all we ask or imagine, according to his power that is at work within us, to him be glory in the church and in Christ Jesus through all generations for ever and ever. Amen" (3:20-21).

Like Joseph, Solomon and the writers of Proverbs and Ecclesiastes, Daniel possesses a gift of wisdom that is different from that of the wise men and sages of his time. Daniel's special and extraordinary wisdom is recalled fifteen hundred years later by a master of verse and drama:

> "A Daniel come to judgment! Yea, a Daniel.
>
> O wise young judge! How I do honor thee!"[129]

In 1 Corinthians, Paul may have been reflecting on Daniel's special type of divine wisdom amid courtly wisdom of the king: "Where is the wise man? Where is the scholar? Where is the philosopher of this age? Has not God made foolish the wisdom of the world? For since in the wisdom of God the world through its wisdom did not know him . . . . Greeks look for wisdom, but we preach Christ crucified . . . . Christ the power of God and the wisdom of God" (1:20-24).

Daniel 3:1-30

A tall gold statue dominates chapter three. By ordering all of his subjects to bow down and worship this ninety foot idol, the king requires the Jews to break the first commandment of the Ten Commandments. In their seeming powerless condition, the Jews of this story find they do possess a power. Not only do despots build pyramids, towers, obelisks, and statues to memorialize their rule but also to emphasize and magnify their personal power and prestige while they are ruling. These objects symbolize the subjugation of others by power and wealth. Readers of this book may recall the rejoicing of the Iraqi people when the large statue of Saddam Hussein was pulled down and dismembered. The two statues, metaphors of their separate times, symbolize the same issues. In the end, the king is humbled by the lack of power his statues have over the Jews who believe in a higher power of creation.

This same powerlessness is manifested in the roaring furnace, **so hot that the flames of the fire killed the soldiers who took up Shadrach, Meshach, and Abednego** (3:22), yet unable to consume the three men thrown into it, **not a hair of their heads singed** (3:27). Though the concept and image were not fully accomplished in that time, the furnace could be interpreted as a metaphor of evil or the underworld. Regardless, human forms of punishment or annihilation are ultimately powerless over the inexhaustible Spirit of God's rule, as in the case of the holocaust. Despite Adolph Hitler's attempts at genocide, some German Jews survived. Their sense of identity was resurrected in the form of the country, Israel. King Louis XIV once asked Voltaire for proof of the existence of God, and the French philosopher immediately responded, "The Jews, my Lord. The Jews." Christians underwent a similar threat to their existence in the early centuries CE and found resilience and hope in the *Book of Revelation*, patterned after the *Book of Daniel*.

Like most apocalyptic literature, *Daniel*, is filled with metaphors. The fiery furnace in *Daniel* is a metaphor for challenge that deepens commitment. As metal is forged, hammered, and shaped in a flaming smelting furnace, so is character developed in those crises that test our mettle and courage. A fourth person appeared with Shadrach, Meshach, and Abednego. If the fiery furnace is a metaphor for challenge to commitment, the appearance of the fourth person is a metaphor for God's presence. In the midst of the challenge or crisis, represented by fire, He is with us. This promise is given in Isaiah: "When you walk through the fire, you will not be burned; the flames will not set you ablaze. For I am the Lord, your God, the Holy One of Israel, your Savior . . . . Since you are precious and honored in my sight, and because I love you . . . ." (43:2-4). According to some interpreters, the fourth person is Jesus or the Holy Spirit. Regardless of the interpretation, metaphorically the Triune God is the fourth person. There was a presence with those three men, just as there was a presence with a lone person on a cross centuries later. In our time of trouble, the biblical truth holds true: God is with us.

Daniel 4:1-37

Chapter four teaches with the knowledge and direction of God, it is possible for political rulers and leaders to be righteous. Three of the great prophets—Daniel, Jonah, Isaiah 19—asserted Assyrian or

Babylonian rulers were not excluded from the kingdom of God simply because of their race or nationality. Through their profound conversion, their authority to rule must shift from themselves to a higher power. They must no longer rule by oppression but by compassion, their justice tempered by mercy.

A theme of righteousness pervades Daniel. Can a person be righteous and mix with the secular world? Or, like the Amish, must individuals separate themselves from the secular world to achieve and/or maintain their righteousness? The Quakers have a more realistic approach. Accepting current realities, they manifest their hope by becoming involved, lobbying, running for office in the hope of God's final transformation. A major lesson in the *Book of Daniel* is that transformation is possible. Rulers can become converted and alter their politics. Though this outcome seems unlikely, if not impossible, for Osama Bin Laden, Kim Jong Il (North Korea), Vladimir Putin (Russia), Ali Khamenei (Iran) and other world leaders considered to be tyrannical. It is our duty as Christians to work and pray for the goal of achieving God's final transformation.

Nebuchadnezzar lifted his eyes to heaven, and he was transformed by God. While focusing on his accomplishments and accumulations of his power, pride separated him from God. His sanity was restored when he was humbled and shifted his vision upward. In the 21st century, many people are troubled because the focus of our vision is on us. As modeled by Nebuchadnezzar, shifting our vision from ourselves to others could diminish our suffering. Jesus said, "I tell you the truth, whatever you did for one of the least of these brothers of mine, you did for me." (Matthew 25:40) Our view is on God when we serve others. Nebuchadnezzar's final comment of the chapter is significant: **And those who walk in pride he is able to humble.**

The lesson of this dream surfaces throughout the Bible. Human pride forgets its source of being, the Creator. We are creatures totally dependent upon our Creator for *everything*. In the beginning God created *everything*. In Genesis, humankind is given dominion over all creatures. Then, dominion turns to domination which leads to exploitation, abuse, neglect, and waste. This happens with rulers, presidents, premiers, and other high officials when their view is on themselves rather than on God.. Antiochus IV Epiphanes is only a symbolic representation of what happens when human pride runs rampant and becomes "vaulting ambition which o'er leaps itself."[130]

Daniel 5:1-30

A major theme of this chapter is the abuse of a people's culture and values by their conquerors. In Daniel 5 an oppressive imperial power is ruthless in its effort to destroy not only a people's identity and value system, but also their faith and religious identity. Belshazaar's rudeness was troubling, but more troubling was his outrageous act of sacrilege, using the vessels from the Jewish Temple at a drunken banquet. Belshazaar profaned God, the God of a vanquished people.

This context becomes unsettling and uncomfortable to Americans when shifted to the North American continent and the Native American Indians. The same occurred to Native Americans in the Pacific Northwest with Captain Cook's desecration of native holy sites. In 1864, the body parts of slain Cheyenne were paraded through downtown Denver following the Sand Creek Massacre which was led by a Christian minister, Rev. Colonel Chivington. Winning is not always enough for the conquerors. They must humiliate their defeated subjects. "Humiliating the conquered," then, helps to sustain the myth of superiority....For modern Christians, Daniel 5 is a call to understand the humiliation of defeated cultures and peoples, and perhaps to work toward reconciliation and restitution so that finally ours can be a society that appreciates and celebrates, the diverse traditions that enrich our life."[131]

As Daniel explained, the message on the wall was a parable of judgment. In this case the judgment is upon Balshazzar, who overstepped his bounds. God's retribution is near at hand. The four words on the wall are measurements of weight, possibly coins. God holds the scales of justice. He weighs the actions of individuals and nations.

Daniel 6:1-28

Non-violent reaction to political injustice is a familiar theme of recent history. Mahatma Gandhi and Martin Luther King, Jr. are modern day Daniels. In particular, Ghandi drew strength from reading the *Book of Daniel* and called him "one of the greatest passive resisters that ever lived."[132] Like the fiery furnace of chapter three, the lions' den becomes a metaphor of unjust punishment and imprisonment. When bad people punish the Jews, then bad things happen to the punishers. The Jews then become a metaphor for the innocent of this world. The lions may serve as metaphors for domestic problems, financial stress, job termination and insecurity, etc. With that interpretation, however, Daniel is not punished for being a Jew but for not bowing down to the emperor. The same is true of his three companions in chapter three and the fiery furnace. They were punished because they refused to bow down and worship the golden statue.

The human trait that drives the plot of the story in chapter six is jealousy. Daniel had been appointed "president" over approximately forty satraps, or administrative divisions. Daniel's efficiency and superior ability had prompted the king to give him the office of Chief Minister of State. The other two presidents felt threatened and became jealous. From the local courthouse to the Oval office, this story is replicated over and over.

Daniel was an honorable man with unquestionable character and integrity. He was innocent of any wrongdoing, but these two presidents who considered him competition were determined to uncover a flaw. In their probe they learned about his religion and his allegiance to his God. When Daniel is accused of crimes and faces being thrown in the lions' den, he went to his rooftop chamber, opened the windows, knelt down, faced Jerusalem and prayed. This gesture was not a momentary move of desperation. It was Daniel's disciplined regular practice of prayer. His custom was to pray three times a day. Later in the New Testament Paul said, "Pray without ceasing"(1 Thessalonians 5:17, *KJV*).

Upon finding Daniel unharmed by the lions, Darius provides a Trinitarian formula on the essence of God. He is a *living* God, the *eternal* God, and the *saving* God. The phrase "living God" is found frequently in the Old Testament. Sharply contrasted with frozen, static idols, God is alive, moving, involved. Throughout Jewish history He is an enduring and everlasting, trustworthy and reliable God who constantly acts on behalf of His people. He is steadfast in his love and faithfulness. He saved Daniel from the lions' den, but He is a *saving* God over all who trust in him. One lesson gleaned from this chapter is found in Darius' Trinitarian view of God in which we can find assurance and hope.

Daniel 7:1-28

Chapter seven makes the transition from the stories of chapters 1-6 to the dreams and visions found in chapters 8-12. Daniel is portrayed as a "visionary," one whose vision penetrates beyond the appearances to core realities; it goes beyond mere occurrences to ultimate meaning. This coincides with the meaning of myth and metaphor described in earlier chapters. Revelations find meaning in symbolic language that is not always initially understood. Dreams and visions, "were a power medium of communication that encouraged the people by drawing on a reservoir of possibilities beyond current realities. It is the nature of faith to look beyond the powers of this world to ask not only about the meaning of these powers, but about their ultimate reality."[133] Imagination plays a significant role in this development of thought and, ultimately, in statements of faith.

The overall message of Chapter seven has been interpreted as follows: Four strange beasts symbolize four regimes that have acted hostilely and viciously against God and His people, must now face judgment. A new age is imminent and a new heavenly kingdom that will destroy the enemies of God's people and set them free is about to emerge. This theme resonates with the Civil Rights Movement of the '60's in America, highlighted by Martin Luther King's, "I Have A Dream," sermon delivered in August of 1963 before over 200,000 gathered along the Mall in Washington. In that speech he said,

> "that in spite of the difficulties and frustrations of
>
> the moment I still have a dream…I have a dream that

one day every valley shall be exalted, every hill and

mountain made low, the rough places will be made

plain, and the crooked places will be made straight,

and the glory of the Lord shall be revealed, and flesh

shall see it together. This is our hope.[134]

Further fulfilling this message is the 2008 election of Barak Obama, an African-American, to the position of President of the United States. Joseph or Daniel could have written that speech. They had dreams that met with disfavor and their dreams were the beginning of the end of their oppression. A plaque on the wall of The Lorraine Motel in Memphis, Tennessee, where Martin Luther King, Jr. was assassinated, encapsulates the similar lives of these three men.

Here comes the dreamer.

Let us kill him and

see what becomes of his dreams.

In his book *The Dawn of Apocalyptic*, scholar Paul Hanson suggested that apocalyptic thinking and literature was ultimately a "flight into the timeless repose of myth."[135] He implies that apocalypticism is a passive waiting for a miraculous intervention from heaven by God who will rush in and free the afflicted and suffering. This interpretation of apocalyptic thought is questionable when one examines the historical experiences of Native American Indians in their struggle with oppression, violence, deportation, and despair. Their own prophets rose up with visions that gave them hope and the will to continue living despite the odds:

One thinks of the famous Ghost Dance religion

across many tribal lines, or the Handsome Lake

religion among the Seneca/Iroquois, of the Indian

Shaker from northwest Indian John Slocum's

> visions. In many cases these visions imagined the intervention of supernatural forces to drive away the European settlers and restore the old ways of tribal life…the result was not passivity or withdrawal—the result was a new approach to reality, a new opening of a way forward for the people.[136]

In historical cases such as the Quakers and Mennonites, apocalyptic thinking became active and transforming. Oppressed groups received inspiration and motivation from *Daniel* and *Revelation.* Religion of this visionary nature can be unpredictable and dangerous. Passions of people can become uncontrollable, but visions do present new possibilities, new ways of circumventing the old traditions of oppression. Christians who hope for a new age and the establishment of God's kingdom in that new age are not irrational visionaries out of touch with reality but represent a "life-style within the world that is built on the vision of God's true kingship and dominion."[137]

The imminent coming kingdom in *Daniel*, as well as *Revelation*, represents a new humanity. It finds its fulfillment in Jesus who said "the time has come . . . kingdom of God is near" (Mark 1:15) Jesus also stated, "the kingdom of God is within you."(Luke 17:21) The implication of these apocalyptic comments is dying to share in the future glory is not required. This new humanity can happen now and becoming part of this new creation is achieved by responding to Christ in repentance, faith, and love. The latter is an action of "doing unto others," and it means to be "in Christ," in the new humanity, the "new creation."

Daniel 8:1-27

Hope is the prominent theme in this last judgment scene. The central question asked is: "How long will it take for the vision to be fulfilled . . . ?" (8:13). The answer, *it will not be long*, infuses hope. The times of persecution, wrath, destruction, genocide, slavery, and oppression do not belong to God's universal rhythm of love. They have their day and, then they are gone. The gospel also promises darkness and evil will not last forever. The time will come when the sheep are separated from the goats (Matthew 25) or the equally powerful story of Lazarus in Luke (16:19-31).

The cry, "How long?" has reverberated through the millennia. "How long, O Lord, how long?" (Psalm 6:3; cf. 80:4; 90:13) "Then I said, 'How long, O Lord?" (Isaiah 6:11) "How long must this go on?" (Habakkuk 2:6) And, from the New Testament comes the question, "How long, Sovereign Lord, holy and true, until you judge the inhabitants of the earth and avenge our blood?" (Revelation 6:10)

Daniel differs from the other prophetic answers to this cry of anguish. Even though he gives a specific time frame there is often a long gap time period for the people to suffer and patiently wait for relief. The following serve as companion scriptures to this segment in Daniel: "For the Lord is a God of justice. Blessed are all who wait for him" (Isaiah 30:18); "But as for me, I watch in hope for the Lord, I wait for the God my Savior; my God will hear me" (Micah 7:7); "I wait for the Lord, my soul waits, and in his word I put my hope. My soul waits for the Lord more than watchmen wait for the morning . . . ." Psalms 130:5-6). The writer of Daniel echoes this theme at the end of the book: "Blessed is the one who waits for and reaches the end of the 1, 335 days" (12:12).

Daniel 9:1-27

In this beautiful and moving confession, told in the first person, to be attuned to God is also to be attuned to each other. This is a communal prayer of confession that includes the entire community of the faithful. All have sinned and fallen short of the glory of God is a prayer reflecting communal ownership of transgressions that does not blame others or cite single individuals, such as a President, or a General. How comfortable we Americans feel shifting responsibility and blame to the Oval Office, the halls of Congress, and the Pentagon. Daniel describes corporate or joint ownership of sin. In essence,

Daniel says, "We asked for this." In asking that God **look with favor on your desolate sanctuary** (9:19) and **forgive**, he is also asking that God act...**do not delay for your city and your people bear your name.** (9:19)

Confession cleanses the soul, but most of us find excuses and deny ownership saying someone else caused the problem. As David O. Dykes puts it, "We live in a no-fault culture in which we are offered "no-fault" insurance and "no-fault" divorce."[138] Daniel did not make excuses. He confessed for himself and the entire nation of Israel. He took responsibility for the corporate sins of the people of Israel who had brought this misery upon themselves.

Following Daniel's confession or admission that he had sinned, he repented and turned away from his sinful ways. The Old Testament meaning of repent is to turn around, to undergo a change of mind that leads to a change of behavior. Confession without repentance is hollow.

Daniel's confession for the nation contained specifics: **we have sinned and done wrong...we have been wicked and have rebelled...We have turned away from your commands and laws** (9:5) **We have not listened to your servants the prophets** (9:6); **we are covered with shame** (9:7); **All Israel has transgressed your law and turned away** (9:11). When we pray, do we confess general sins or do we cite specifics? Being specific in our confession and our repentance is more likely to produce a change of mind that leads to a change in behavior.

While Daniel is still in prayer, Gabriel comes to him and the theme of prayer surfaces again. Some suggest Gabriel's sudden appearance means Daniel's prayer was answered instantly, yet reality tells us this is not always true. People of faith pray with the expectation their prayer will be answered. Mature and seasoned people of faith pray with an understanding and acceptance their prayer will be answered though the answer may not always be the one desired.

Daniel 10:1-21

Chapter ten can be summarized in one verse: **Do not be afraid...be strong.** (10:19) The Lord is bracing and strengthening

Daniel for spiritual warfare. Some scholars argue "the entire book of Daniel is a call to arms for spiritual warfare, or a training ground for serving in God's 'court' while living in the human world. The weapons of war and the training for service both involve the same thing: knowledge of the truth."[139] The problem with this interpretation is its focus on "knowledge of the truth." The first heresy faced by the early church was Gnosticism, which was heavily endowed with apocalyptic thought. A key component of Gnosticism is salvation by knowledge, not by grace and faith. Gnosticism has surfaced again in contemporary Fundamentalism where the emphasis appears to fall on "knowing Jesus" and not "faith in Jesus." This might sound like a matter of semantics, but the suggestion that knowledge is the weapon of spiritual warriors infers that knowledge saves. In reality, faith in God's grace is the primary weapon. Paul must have understood this when he wrote, " . . . put on faith and love as a breastplate, and the hope of salvation as a helmet" (1 Thessalonians 5:8). In his description of preparing for spiritual warfare, the Pauline author of Ephesians says, "Put on the full armor of God…Stand firm then, with the belt of truth buckled around your waist, with the breastplate of righteousness in place, and with your feet fitted with the readiness that comes from the gospel of peace. In addition to all, take up the shield of faith . . . the helmet of salvation and the sword of the Spirit, which is the word of God. And pray in the Spirit on all occasions with all kinds of prayers and requests . . . always keep on praying" (6:13, 14-18). Perhaps knowledge is not mentioned because of its association with Gnosticism in those early stages of the church's existence.

The key emphasis of this chapter is on the words, echoed centuries later in Paul's letters, **Do not be afraid . . . be strong.** Several days before his untimely death, the great German theologian Paul Tillich spoke to a group of students at Emory University's Candler School of Theology. At the conclusion of his talk, one student asked this poignant question: Professor Tillich, what does God expect of us?" Tillich's response was immediate. In his strong Teutonic bass voice, his fists clenched and coming down on the lectern, "To be strong," he said. "To be strong."

Jesus was constantly telling his disciples to, "Fear not . . . . Some examples in scripture include, but are not limited to, Matthew 10:26; 10:28; 10:31; 14:27; Mark 5:36; 6:50; Luke 5:10; 8:50; 12:04; 12: 07; 12:32; John 12:15

Daniel 11 and 12

The final two chapters of Daniel are about the end of the reign of Antiochus IV Epiphanes and the end of time, the eschaton or last day. Chapter eleven is a lesson in history written with the confidence, "that in all things God works for the good of those who love him..." (Romans 8:28). In chapter twelve, the writer predicts the end of time to the exact day. One must consider the historical context of the book and its purpose: to give hope to the Jews and encourage them to endure. A couple of centuries later, a man from Nazareth would warn against this type of prophecy. In the thirteenth chapter of Mark, often called the "little apocalypse," Jesus says, "No one knows about that hour or day, not even the angels in heaven, nor the Son, but only the Father...you do not know when the time will come" (13:32-33). Jesus' words are "Be on guard . . . be alert . . . keep watch" (13:33, 35) Several of the parables of Jesus emphasize the theme of readiness for the last day: The wise and foolish virgins (Matthew 25:1-13), The Great Banquet (Matthew 22:1-10; Luke 14:15-24), The Guest without a Wedding Garment (Matthew 22:11-13), The Two Houses (Matthew 7:24-27; Luke 6:47-49).

The last two chapters of Daniel are also about the Final Judgment. There is a tendency within some theological interpretations of the New Testament and the message of Jesus of Nazareth to focus on the mercy of God, with limited emphasis on his judgment. Often we forget God holds out two hands, one of mercy and the other of judgment. God, the Ancient of Days, is the only One who can judge. When we mortals judge, we break the first commandment. A dominant theme in the message of Christ was, "Do not judge or you will be judged." (Matthew 7:1)

The final chapters of Daniel form a bridge to the New Testament. The "son of man" concept, messianic hope, and resurrection are absorbed and expanded by the New Testament writers. The Book of

Daniel becomes the seedbed for the growing belief in life after death. The Hebrew mind did not conceive of life beyond the grave, only a shadowy existence in Sheol, the gloomy land to which a man's soul descended with no chance of return (2 Samuel 12:23; Job 7:9) and no chance of knowledge. Where Daniel ends, the very core of the Christian faith begins with the resurrection of Jesus Christ, "the first-fruits of those who have fallen asleep" (1 Corinthians 15:20).

QUESTIONS FOR FURTHER STUDY AND DISCUSSION

1. What are the things we as Christians today must resist to maintain our spiritual identity and values? In other words, what **king's food and wine** are we being offered today by modern "kings" that we should resist?
2. In line with the question above, is purity the most effective, appropriate, and/or realistic way of protecting our Christian values and presenting Christ to the world?
3. If we are "one nation under God," are other nations as well under God. In other words, do all rulers rule with God's permission, as indicated in chapter 4 of Daniel? (cf. John 19:10-11; Romans 13:6-7)
4. Within the secular political systems of world states, can a ruler be righteous?
5. Name other instances in which defeated peoples have been humiliated and their religious sites and symbols desecrated.
6. What can Christians learn about Hope from the Book of Daniel?

Endnotes

1 Joseph Campbell and Bill Moyers, *The Power of Myth*, (New York: Doubleday, 1988), p. 18.

2 *The Power of Myth.*, p. 13

3 William Shakespeare, *The Tempest*, Act IV, Scene 1, in *The Complete Works of Shakespeare*, ed. Hardin Craig, (Chicago: Scott, Foresman and Company, 1961,) p. 1266.

4 (Edinburgh: T & T Clark, 1964).

5 Dietrich Bonhoeffer, *Creation and Fall*, (New York: The MacMillan Company, 1959), 75.

6 Ibid., 66.

7 The genealogy of Matthew extends back only to David.

8 *Power of Myth*, 50.

9 *Creation and Fall*, 76.

10 In 1 Samuel 5:11 God repents over his decision to have made Saul. One word for repent in Hebrew is *nacham*, which means to turn around, to change. According to *The HarperCollins Bible Dictionary*, "The most important aspect of OT repentance, however, is contained in the Hebrew word *shub*, which expresses the idea of turning back, retracing one's steps in order to return to the right way," (San Francisco: HarperSanFrancisco, 1996), 924.

11 *Power of Myth*, 34.

12 *Creation and Fall*, 78.

13 Ibid., 79.

14 *Creation and Fall*, p. 60. Joseph Campbell gives it a different twist: "When man ate of the fruit of the first tree, the tree of the knowledge of good and evil, he was expelled from the Garden. The Garden is the place of unity, nonduality of male and female, good and evil, God and human beings. You eat the duality and you are on the way out." *Power of Myth*, 107.

15 Bonhoeffer, 75.

16 Gerhard von Radd, *Old Testament Theology, Vol I,* Trans. D. M. G. Stalker, (New York: Harper & Row: 1962), 155.

17 Bonhoeffer, 93.

18 Thompson, Francis. "The Hound of Heaven" in *The Norton Anthology of English Literature, Vol. 2.* (New York: Norton & Norton Company, Inc., 1968), 1210.

19 *Creation and Fall*, 93.

20 Alfred Lord Tennyson, "In Memoriam," from *The Works of Tennyson*, (London: C. Kegan Paul & Co., 1878), vi.

[21] The term "Garden of Gethsemane" does not appear in the New Testament. In two passages in the Gospel of John (*KJV*) a garden is mentioned in relation to Jesus' last hours (18:1; 18:26) but Gethsemane is not. In the *NIV* "garden" in these two instances is translated "olive grove." In Matthew (26:36) and Mark (14:32) Gethsemane is mentioned but it is not called a garden. The word "Gethsemane" translates "wine press" from the Hebrew.

[22] *Creation and Fall* , 94.

[23] *The Interpreter's Bible,* (Nashville: Abingdon Press, 1952), 531.

[24] *The New Interpreter's Bible,* Vol I, (Nashville: Abingdon Press, 1994), 397.

[25] The statistics in this segment were obtained from the website animalcruelty.com.

[26] The Tower of Babel is generally understood as a temple or ziggurat. Ziggaruts held an important place in ancient history. Archaeological evidence of ziggurats indicates they had a square base with stepped tiers leading to a sanctuary at the top. The ziggarut of Marduk, constructed in the first millennium was known as "the house that is the foundation of heaven and earth." *HarperCollins Bible Dictionary*, 1244.

[27] Gerhard von Radd, *Old Testament Theology, Vol. I,* 163.

[28] Cf. Hermann Gunkel, *Genesis,* (Göttingen: Vandenhoeck & Ruprecht, 1922), 92-94 and John Skinner, *Genesis,* (New York: Charles Scribners, 1910), 223-224.

[29] Some scholars believe this was an independent story circulating at the time to explain the origins of different tribes, peoples, and nations. Cf. Bernhard W. Anderson, *Understanding the Old Testament,* (Englewood Cliffs, New Jersey: Prentice-Hall, Inc., 1966) and *The Interpreter's Bible,* (Nashville: Abingdon Press, 1952).

[30] Gunkel notes, "...one variant of the legend of Babel asks the origin of the difference of languages and the city of Babel, the other wants to know the source of the distribution of races and also of a certain ancient structure." Hermann Gunkel, *The Legends of Genesis*, (New York: Schocken Books, 1964), 77.

[31] William Shakespeare, *Troilus and Cressidat,* Ed. Hardin Craig, (*The Complete Works of Shakespeare.* Chicago: Scott, Foresman and Company, 1961), 878.

[32] *The Interpreter's Bible,* 564.

[33] William Shakespeare, *The Tempest,* Act IV, Scene 1, in *The Complete Works of Shakespeare,* ed. Hardin Craig, (Chicago: Scott, Foresman and Company, 1961,), 1266.

[34] Percy Bysshe Shelley, "Ozymandias," *English Romantic Poets.* ed. James Stephens, Edwin L. Beck, Royall H. Snow, (New York: American Book Company, 1961), 417.

[35] Fyodor Dostoyevsky, *The Brothers Karamazov,* Trans. Constance Garnett, (New York: New American Library), 233.

[36] *New Interpreter's Bible,* p. 412.

[37] Robert Frost, "Mending Wall," *A College Book of Modern Verse,* ed. James K. Robinson and Walter B. Rideout, (Evanston, Illinois: Row, Peterson and Company, 1958), p. 222.

[38] *The New Interpreters Bible, Vol. I,* 413.

[39] Bruce Feiler, *Abraham: Journey to the Heart of Three Faiths,* (New York: HarperCollins Publishers, 2002), 40.

[40] *New Interpreter's Bible, Vol. I.,* 497.

[41] Walter Brueggemann, *Genesis,* (Atlanta: John Knox Press, 1982), 187.

[42] Bruce Feiler, *Abraham,* p. 9.

[43] Feiler, 44.

[44] *The New International Lesson Annual,* (Nashville: Abingdon Press, 2004), 133.

[45] Cf. Ray Raphael's *The First American Revolution,* (New York: The New Press, 2002).

[46] (New York: Doubleday & Company, Inc., 1954)

[47] In 2 Kings 3:27 scripture states the king of Moab "took his first-born son who was to succeed him as king, and offered him as a sacrifice on the city wall."

[48] Søren Kierkegaard, *Fear and Trembling,* 35.

[49] Feiler, 208.

[50] Quoted from Feiler, 199-200.

[51] *Understanding the Old Testament,* 8.

[52] R. Alan Cole, *Exodus: An Introduction and Commentary,* (Downers Grove, IL: Inter-Varsity Press, 1973), 17.

[53] *New Interpreter's Bible, Vol. I,* 445.

[54] Genesis, Exodus, and the remaining books of the Pentateuch—Leviticus, Deuteronomy, and Numbers—comprise the Torah which is the complete system of biblical law, often referred to as Mosaic Law.

[55] *Interpreter's Bible,* 875.

[56] Carl van Doren, *Benjamin Franklin,* (New York: Viking Press, 1938), 553.

[57] Robert Frost, *Frost: The Poet and His Poetry,* "Two Roads," (New York: Bantam Books, 1969), 70.

[58] Bryan Binns, *Abraham Lincoln,* (New York: E. P. Dutton & Co., 1907), 77.

[59] *New Interpreter's Bible,* 796.

[60] *De Carne Christi, 5.*

[61] 853.

[62] The first two commandments are interrelated and for that reason combined by some denominations.

[63] (New York: Harper & Row, 1965).

[64] (New York: Charles C. Scribner's Sons, 1970.).

[65] Bill Moyers in *Power of Myth,* Joseph Campbell, 111.

[66] *Power of Myth,* 22.

[67] Joe E. Morris, *Systematic Jury Selection in Mississippi: A Practical Appro* (Jackson, MS: Hederman Brothers Printers, 1997).

[68] *The Collected Works of G. K. Chesterton,* (San Francisco: Ignatius Press, 1986), 3

[69] *Power of Myth.* 7.

[70] Khaled Hosseini, *The Kite Runner*, (New York: Riverhead Books, 2003), 17-1

[71] 1109.

[72] 853

[73] *Ruth* is one of the books of the Ketuvim, ("Writings" of the Old Testame "Nehemiah attempted to put an end to all marriages of Jews with non-Jews on ground of preserving the original commandment of God (Neh. 10-13; cf. E 9:1-3) Many scholars have taken the book of Ruth as a response to this spec attempt to enforce the separation of Israel from other peoples."*Interpreter's Dictionary of the Bible, Vol. R-Z,* (Nashville: Abingdon Press, 1962), 133.

[74] *Vol 2*, Kathleen A. Robertson Farmer, (Nashville: Abingdon Press, 1998), 894.

[75] *Interpreter's Dictionary of the Bible, Vol. R-Z*, 132.

[76] *Interpreter's Dictionary of the Bible, Vol. R-Z*, 132.

[77] *Ibid.*.

[78] The term entered our vocabulary in the 1990's with the conflicts in the Balkan Peninsula.

[79] *The Books of Ruth, Esther, Eccesiastes, the Song of Songs, Lamentations,* (London: Cambridge University Press: 1975), 8.

[80] In the story of Goliath, David arrives in camp and Saul questions him about his identity. (1 Samuel 17:55-58) However, in the preceding passage (1 Samuel 16:17-22), David plays the harp for Saul.

[81] Strands of J and E weave in and out of the narrative and a Deuteronomic editor also had a hand in the redaction. (Cf. Martin Noth, *The Deuteronomic History*, (Sheffield, England: JSOT Press, 1981). "A compilation of earlier accounts, which may have included a life of Samuel, a history of the ark, and the accounts of the inauguration of the monarchy as well as annals of David's reign, would have been put together by an editor, probably during the exile." (Joyce G. Baldwin, *1 & 2 Samuel*, (Downers Grove, Illinois: InterVarsity Press, 1988) An early source, sometimes referred to as the "Saul" source may have been an eye-witness account of events occurring in the mid-tenth century BCE. A source, referred to by some scholars as the "Samuel" source dates between 750 and 650 BCE. This writer is dogmatic and disapproves of a monarchy. Another source is Deuteronomic material dating from 550 BCE. Parts were written following the Exile (500-400 BCE) (cf. 2 Samuel 7; 1 Samuel 2:1-10; and 2 Samuel 23:1-7. cf. Warren W. Jackson, *Legend, Myth, and History in the Old Testament*, (Wellesley Hill, Massachusetts: Independent School Press, 1970).

[82] One source was a pre-exilic edition or redaction of the Deuteronomic history probably prepared in the reign of Hezekiah. A second edition heralded Josiah as

the new David. Some scholars contend much of the work was written in exile and others place authorship of certain passages within Palestine. Literary analysis of 1 and 2 Kings is inexact. Wiseman, Donald J. *1 and 2 Kings*. (Downers Grove, Illinois: InterVarsity Press, 1993).

[83] *The Message of Chronicles*, (Downers Grove, Illinois: InterVarsity Press, 1987), p. 13.

[84] *The Interpreter's Bible*, 771.

[85] 2 Samuel 21:19 credits the feat to one Elhanan. A latter attempt to harmonize this inconsistency is made by 1 Chronicles 20:5.

[86] *A History of Israel* ,(London: SCM Press LTD, 1966), 171.

[87] Israel Finklestein and Neil Asher Silberman,. *David and Solomon,* (New York: Free Press, 2006.), 7.

[88] In 1867 a water shaft was discovered by British explorer Charles Warren. The shaft may have been first hewn in the Middle Bronze Age (2000-1550 BCE) and probably expanded during the reign of Hezekiah. Whether tunnel was actually in existence when David took Jerusalem or was part of folklore developed at a later time is difficult to determine.

[89] Bright, *History of Israel*, 179.

[90] Specific details are provided in Exodus 25:10-30 and 37:1-9.The Ark may have been originally housed in the "tent of meeting" and later transferred to the more elaborate Tabernacle though there is no evidence it was ever covered by the "tent of meeting." They are brought together when a tent was placed over the Tabernacle (Exodus 36:14).

[91] In Exodus, the specifications and instructions for building the Tabernacle (25-30; 35-40) are clearly indicated. It was to be a rectangular enclosure, "hung with curtains supported on poles, some 145 feet (44m) long, 72 feet (22m) wide, and 7 feet (2.2 meters) high (Exod. 27:18). Within this area was another, also hung with curtains and portioned by a veil. Behind the veil was the Holy of Holies which contained the Ark. In front of the veil was an altar of incense and 7-branched lampstand and a table for the bread of the Presence (25:30) Outside the tabernacle was a courtyard which contained an altar of burnt offering and laver. (30:18) Each time the Hebrews moved, the Tabernacle was disassembled by the Levites and reassembled at the next camp. In the Book of Numbers it states the Israelites camped around the Tabernacle in a set order.(Numbers 1:51) In essence, the Tabernacle was a portable sanctuary and a probable "retrojection of the of the Jerusalem Temple to the wilderness epoch, in accordance with the Priestly view that all Israel's religious institutions originated at that time, but with the knowledge that a permanent building did not exist before the settlement in Canaan." (*HarperCollins Bible Dictionary,* 1088) The structure and contents of the Tabernacle have raised doubts among some that it ever existed, at least with these elaborate specifications. The "tent of meeting," however, described in an

early Exodus passage (33:7-11) has more plausibility in the Priestly account. A single individual could ditch and pitch a tent without assistance. The "tent of meeting" was also outside the camp and not in the center like the Tabernacle, and served a different function.

[92] *HarperCollins Bible Dictionary,* 70.

[93] Joyce G. Baldwin, *1 & 2 Samuel* (Downers Grove, Illinois: InterVarsity Press, 1988), 217.

[94] *The New Interpreter's Bible, vol. II,* (Nashville: Abingdon Press, 1998), 1114.

[95] *The New Interpreter's Bible, vol. II,* 1235.

[96] von Radd, Vol II, 311.

[97] Ibid.

[98] Quoted in the NY Times, October, 1973.

[99] Anderson, *Understanding the Old Testament,* 148.

[100] *Ibid.*

[101] *The New Interpreter's Bible, Vol. III,* (Nashville: Abingdon Press, 1999).

[102] 151. "Ben Sirach, writing ca. 180 B.C.E., does not mention Esther or Mordecai in his list of heroes of Israel. The earliest witness to the existence of the book of Esther is probably the LXX translation (at the end of the second century B.C.E." (Ibid.) Walter Brueggemann tends to agree. He admits the narrative is filled with familiarity of Persian culture and politics, but argues, "the story in the book of Esther may well date later in the Hellenistic period." *An Introduction to the Old Testament,* (Louisville, Kentucky: Westminster John Knox Press, 2003), 343.

[103] *New Interpreter's Bible.*

[104] Ibid.

[105] Brueggemann, *An Introduction to the Old Testament,* 343.

[106] "While the book is rooted in historical, political, and cultural reality, critical scholars do not regard it as historical reportage, but as novelistic imagination rooted in historical awareness. This critical judgment means that the book requires a certain mode of reading that is committed to imaginative instruction of a world of Jewish courage through narrative performance." Brueggemann, 343-44.

[107] *New Interpreter's Bible* and *HarperCollins Bible Dictionary,* (San Francisco: HarperSanFrancisco, 1996.)

[108] Wesley J. Fuerst, *The Books of Ruth, Esther, Ecclesiastes, The Song of Songs, and Lamentations,* (London: Cambridge University Press, 1975), *New Interpreters Bible, and HarperCollins Bible Dictionary.*

[109] *New Interpreter's Bible,* 855.

[110] 309.

[111] *Interpreter's Dictionary of the Bible,* 150.

[112] Ibid.

[113] Ibid.,151.

[114] *Ruth, Esther, Ecclesiastes, The Song of Songs and Lamentations,* 41.

[115] Ibid.
[116] Fuerst, 40.
[117] Brueggemann, 344.
[118] THE INTERNATIONAL LESSON ANNUAL, 359.
[119] *The Norton Anthology of English Literature, vol. 2,* (New York: W. W. Norton & Company, 1968), 1210.
[120] Joachim Jeremias, *Rediscovering the Parables,* (New York: Charles Scriber's Sons, 1966), 123.
[121] *New Interpreter's Bible,* 525.
[122] *The International Lesson* Annual, 361.
[123] *New Interpreter's Bible,* 526.
[124] *Old Testament Theology,* 292.
[125] *Understanding the Old Testament.*
[126] *The HarperCollins Bible Dictionary,* 930.
[127] Other examples found outside of the Bible in the Apocrypha include *1* and *2 Enoch, 4 Ezra, 2* and *3 Baruch, Jubilees,* and the *Apocalypse of Abraham.* Fragments of *1 Enoch* were discovered in the Dead Sea Scrolls along with Gnostic apocalypses including *The Coptic Apocalypse of Peter, The Apocalypse of Paul, The Apocalypse of Peter.FTN* James Robinson, ed. *The Nag Hammadi Library in English.* 3rd ed. New York: Harper and Row, 1988. For a complete list of the entire library see James Robinson, *The Nag Hammadi Library* in English, 4th rev.
[128] No other book in the Old Testament mentions a belief in resurrection or deals with the last day, or eschaton.
[129] Grand Rapids, Michigan: Kregel Publications, 2004), 24.
[130] *The Affluent Society,* (New York: The New York American Library, 1958).
[131] William Shakespeare, *The Merchant of Venice,* Act IV, Scene 1, ed. Hardin Craig, (Chicago: Scott, Foresman and Company, 1961), 525.
[132] William Shakespeare, *Macbeth,* Act I, Scene 7, ed. Hardin Craig, 1051.
[133] *New Interpreter's Bible,* 85.
[134] Ibid. 94.
[135] *New Interpreter's* Bible, 106.
[136] Speech delivered on August 28, 1963.
[137] (Minneapolis: Fortress Press, 1986), p. 30.
[138] *New Interpreter's Bible,* p. 107.
[139] Ibid. p. 108.
[140] Character out of Chaos, 108.
[141] New Interpreter's Bible, p. 151.

Bibliography

Anderson, Bernard. *Understanding the Old Testament*. Englewood Cliffs, New Jersey: Prentice-Hall, Inc., 1966.

Baldwin, Joyce G. *1 & 2 Samuel*. Downers Grove, Illinois: InterVarsity Press, 1988.

Binns, Bryan. *Abraham Lincoln*. New York: E. P. Dutton & Co., 1907.

Bonhoeffer, Dietrich. *Creation and Fall*. New York: The MacMillan Company, 1966

Bright, John. *A History of Israel*. London: SCM Press LTD, 1966.

Brueggemann, Walter. *An Introduction to the Old Testament*. John Knox Press, 2003.

Brueggemann, Walter. *Genesis*. Atlanta: John Knox Press, 1982.

Buber, Martin. *I and Thou*. New York: Charles C. Scribner's Sons, 1970.

Campbell, Joseph and Moyers, Bill. *Power of Myth* New York: Doubleday, 1988.

Chesterton, Gilbert Keith. *The Collected Works of G. K. Chesterton*. San Francisco: Ignatius Press, 1986.

Cole, R. Alan. *Exodus: An Introduction and Commentary*. Downers Grove, IL: Inter-Varsity Press, 1973.

Dostoyevsky, Fyodor. *The Brothers Karamazov*, Trans. Garnett, Constance. New York, New American Library, 1957.

Dykes, David O. *Character out Of Chaos*.

Farmer, Kathleen A. Robertson. "The Book of Ruth." *The New Interpreter's Bible, Vo. II*. Nashville: Abingdon Press, 1998.

Feiler, Bruce. *Abraham: Journey to the Heart of Three Faiths*. New York: HarperCollins Publishers, 2002.

Finklestein, Israel and Silberman, Neil Asher. *David and Solomon*. New York: Free Press, 2006.

Frost, Robert. "Mending Wall." *A College Book of Modern Verse*. Ed. James K. Robinson and Walter B. Rideout. Evanston, Illinois: Row, Peterson and Company, 1958.

Frost, Robert. *Frost: The Poet and His Poetry*. New York: Bantam Books, 1969.

Fuerst, Wesley J., *The Books of Ruth, Esther, Ecclesiastes, Song of Songs, Lamentations*, (London: Cambridge University Press, 1975).

Galbraith, John Kenneth. *The Affluent Society.* New York: The New York American Library, 1958.

Gunkel, Hermann. *Genesis.* Göttingen: Vandenhoeck & Ruprecht, 1922.

_____. *The Legends of Genesis.* Trans. W. H. Carruth. New York: Schocken Books, 1964.

Hanson, Paul. *The Dawn of Apocalypse.* (Minneapolis: Fortress Press, 1986).

HarperCollins Bible Dictionary. San Francisco: HarperSanFrancisco, 1996.

Hosseini, Khaled. *The Kite Runner.* New York: Riverhead Books, 2003.

Interpreter's Dictionary of the Bible, Vol. E-J. Nashville: Abingdon Press, 1962.

_____, *Vol. K-Q.* Nashville: Abingdon Press, 1962

_____, *Vol. R-Z,* (Nashville: Abingdon Press, 1962

Jackson, Warren W. *Legend, Myth, and History in the Old Testament.* Wellesley Hills, MA: Independent School Press, 1970.

Jeremias, Joachim. *Rdiscovering the Parables.* New York: Charles Schribner's Sons, 1966.

Kierkegaard, Søren. *Fear and Trembling.* New York: Doubleday & Company, Inc., 1954.

Kierkegaard, Søren. *Purity Of Heart Is To Will One Thing.* New York: Harper & Row, 1965.

Morris, Joe E. *Revival of the Gnostic Heresy: Fundamentalism.* New York: Palgrave MacMillan, 2008.

New York Times, October, 1973.

Noth, Martin. *The Deuteronomic History.* Sheffield, England: JSOT Press, 1981.

Raphael, Ray. *The First American Revolution.* New York: The New Press, 2002.

Shakespeare, William. *The Tempest.* Ed. Hardin Craig. *The Complete Works of Shakespeare.* Chicago: Scott, Foresman and Company, 1961.

_____. *Macbeth.* Ed. Hardin Craig. *The Complete Works of Shakespeare.* Chicago:
Scott, Foresman and Company, 1961.

_____. *The Merchant of Venice.* Ed. Hardin Craig. *The Complete Works of Shakespeare.* Chicago: Scott, Foresman and Company, 1961.

Shelley, Percy Bysshe. "Ozymandias." *English Romantic Poets.* Ed. James Stephens, Edwin L. Beck, Royall H. Snow, New York: American Book Company, 1961.

Skinner, John. *Genesis.* New York: Charles Scribners, 1910.

Stewart, James S. *The Gates of New Life.* Edinburgh: T & T Clark, 1964.

Tennyson, Alfred Lord, "In Memoriam," from *The Works of Tennyson.* London: C. Kegan Paul & Co., 1878.

Tertullian. *De Carne Christ*, 5.

The Interpreter's Bible. Nashville: Abingdon Press, 1952.

The New International Lesson Annual. Nashville: Abingdon Press, 2004.

The New Interpreter's Bible, Vol. I. Nashville: Abingdon Press, 1994.

The New Interpreter's Bible, Vol. II. Nashville: Abingdon Press, 1998.

The New Interpreter's Bible, Vol. III. Nashville: Abingdon Press, 1999.

The Norton Anthology of English Literature, Vol 2. New York: W. W. Norton & Co., 1968.

Thompson, Francis. "The Hound of Heaven" in *The Norton Anthology of English Literature, Vol. 2.* New York: Norton & Norton Company, Inc., 1968.

Van Dorn, Carl. *Benjamin Franklin.* New York: Viking Press, 1938.

Von Radd, Gerhard. *Old Testament Theology, Vol. I.* Trans. D. M. G. Stalker. New York: Harper & Row, 1962.

Von Radd, Gerhard. *Old Testament Theology, Vol II.* Trans. D. M. G. Stalker. New York: Harper & Row, 1965.

Wilcock, Michael. *The Message of Chronicles.* Downers Grove, Illinois: InterVarsity Press, 1987.

Wiseman, Donald J. *1 and 2 Kings.* Downers Grove, Illinois: InterVarsity Press, 1993.

CPSIA information can be obtained at www.ICGtesting.com
Printed in the USA
LVOW05s1110010414

379822LV00012B/125/P